BEGINNER'S
GUIDE TO
FLYTYING

Chris Mann & Terry Griffiths

MERLIN UNWIN BOOKS

First published in Great Britain by Merlin Unwin Books, 1999
Reprinted in 2002, 2005 and 2009

ISBN 978 1 873674 39 0

Published by

Merlin Unwin Books Ltd
7 Corve Street, Ludlow
Shropshire SY8 1DB, U.K.

www.merlinunwin.co.uk

British Library Cataloguing-in-publication Data:
A catalogue record of this book is available from the British Library.

CONTENTS

Continued .....

CONTENTS

INTRODUCTION

The **Beginner's Guide to Flytying** is just that – a **beginner's** guide. In order to avoid the pitfall of assuming that you already know something about flytying, I have gone right back to the beginning and made no assumptions about what you may already know. I have started by presuming that you know absolutely nothing. For those of you who have some knowledge already, reading the first sections will do no harm, and you may find some aspects interesting.

In this book I shall lead you through all the procedures necessary for you to tie a vast range of flies successfully. I shall start from the very beginning, explaining about tools, hooks and materials, and lead on to sections which explain the basic skills of flytying. These are the building blocks on which all successful flytying is based. The techniques learned here will stand you in good stead for all your future flytying. Even the most complex flies are based on these basic skills.

Tying your own flies is not just a hobby. For the keen fly fisherman who wishes to improve his chances of catching fish, it is a necessity. Many of the most successful new fly patterns are not available from commercial sources and the quality and correctness of the dressings that *are* available can vary wildly. Tying your own flies puts you in the driving seat. You can try new variations of standard patterns or develop your own specials to suit the problems posed by your own local waters. Experimentation is the key, but to do this you need a good grounding in basic tying techniques. This book is intended to answer that need.

Chris Mann

A GLOSSARY OF FLYTYING TERMS

Abdomen:
The rear part of the fly body behind the thorax of a nymph or imitation of a real fly, is often referred to as the abdomen.

Butt:
A turn or two of fluffy material, normally herl, which is used to divide body sections or to divide the tail from the body of a fly.

Cape:
A part of the neck of a bird which consists of the feathers (hackles) still attached to the skin. The best way of buying hackles.

Cheeks:
Small feathers tied each side of the main wing of a fly. Some flies have both cheeks and eyes. If so, the eyes are the smaller feathers.

Dubbing:
The art of creating a fly body by spreading fibres or hair around the tying thread and then wrapping the thread around the hook shank. Also the material used to do this.

Eye:
This can mean the imitation of real eyes or it can mean the use of small feathers tied either side of the main wing which are intended to act as attraction target point.

Quill:
A feather normally from the wing of a bird. Also a single stalk of a feather such as a peacock eye which is used to form a segmented fly body.

Ribbing:
A spiral overwrap along a body. Usually of tinsel or wire but other materials such as thread or wool may be used.

Saddle:
The rump of a hen or cockerel. Hackles from this part of the bird are longer than those from a neck cape. Good for palmered hackles.

Slip:
A group of married fibres taken from a quill. Normally used for winging but can also be used for forming wing cases.

Tag:
That part of a fly which lies behind and underneath the tail. Some flies have a few turns of tinsel or floss (or both) or a bunch of fibres which are tied in before the tail.

Thorax:
That part of a fly body which lies between the abdomen and head of a fly. Normally applicable to flies or nymphs that attempt to imitate a real insect.

Throat:
A hackle which lies under the hook shank just behind the head. Can also be called a beard hackle.

Tinsel:
Originally metallic thread. Modern versions are mainly non-tarnishing plastics which come in a variety of colours and forms: flat, oval, etc. Mainly used for ribbing but flat tinsel may also be used to form bodies.

Tippets:
Feather fibres taken from the neck crest of a pheasant. Used mainly for tails but may also be used as winging materials.

Wing:
The part of a fly which is tied in above the hook shank, sloping backwards over the body. On imitations of adult flies this may represents a real wing, otherwise it simply means materials tied in this position.

Wing Buds:
A bunch of fibres (hair, floss or feather) used on nymphs and emergers to suggest the wings emerging from the wing case.

Wing Case:
The part of a fly which imitates the wing case of a nymph.

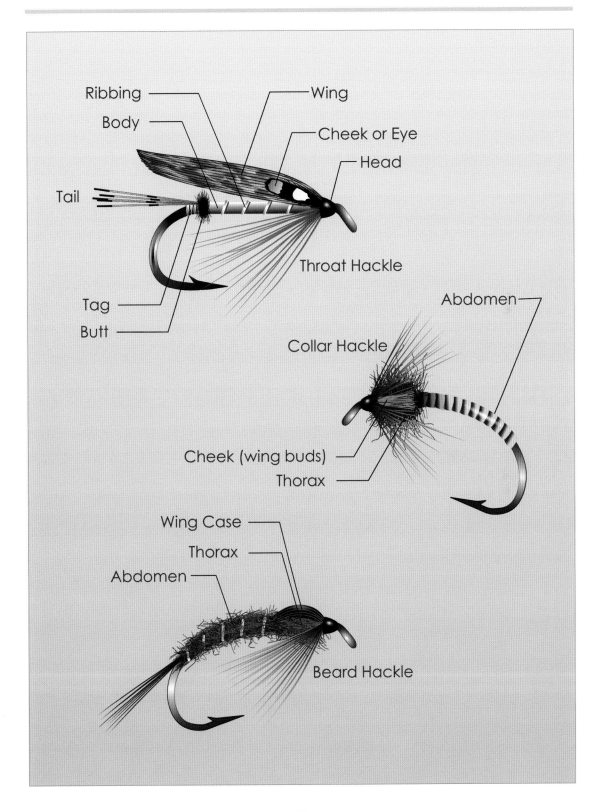

STRUCTURE OF THE BOOK

Now a word or two about the structure of the book. We have tried to lay things out in a straightforward and logical manner.

The first chapter concerns itself with the tools that you will need to start flytying. In common with many other hobbies and sports, there are thousands of gadgets and gimmicks available. Some of these are useful, many are not. We will leave you to make your own collection of such things, and have concentrated on a basic set of tools which are needed to dress flies successfully.

The materials that you will need to obtain in order to dress flies are also covered in this section. Using our recommended materials list you will be able to cover several hundred different patterns. The materials suggested have been carefully chosen to offer you the widest range, whilst at the same time offering you the best value for money

Other, additional materials required for specific flies can always be added at a later date. Naturally we have ensured that a comprehensive list of the materials needed to tie the sample patterns in this book is included (see page 12).

The second chapter covers all the various aspects of the basic skills of flytying. This includes such things as making and ribbing fly bodies, hackling and winging. Each subject is covered separately in some detail with instructions and accompanying illustrations.

The techniques shown on these pages are absolutely vital for the further development of your fly dressing skills. If your basic tying technique is not sound then you will encounter many problems when you attempt more advanced techniques later on.

The last part of the book is a series of dressing instructions for twelve contrasting flies.

The flies have been carefully selected to show a range of tying techniques. Where two patterns were available, both of which fulfilled the same function, we have chosen the pattern which best illustrated a particular tying feature. Again, we have taken great care with the layout so that the words and pictures are always opposite each other on a double page spread. You will need both hands to tie the fly – turning pages backwards and forwards doesn't help. Lay the book open at the correct page, and you have a bench tying manual which you can have in front of you as you are working on the fly.

Throughout the book you will also find pages headed **Tricks of the Trade**. These pages are full of useful supplementary information, advice and tips that you will find useful. The informations often extends and elaborates on points made in the tying instructions, as well as giving you information about a range of related topics.

TOOLS OF THE TRADE

In order to tie flies you will need a basic set of tools. The following list comprises the essentials, plus some additional, optional bits which make the job easier .

Scissors
The most important part of the kit: too much care cannot be taken when choosing scissors. Good scissors will have fine tapered tips, not too long in the blade, and be sharp through to the tips. Some scissors nowadays come with serrated blades: these are a distinct bonus when clipping fine strands of fur or feather. It is an advantage for the finger loops to be large, so that they can be picked up and put down easily without having to wrestle them off. Those suitable for flytying need be no more than 3-4 inches long overall. It is strongly recommended that you have a couple of pairs of scissors, one pair for the fine work with silk, fur and feather, and a second pair for heavy duty cutting of tinsels and wire.

Vice
This will be your biggest single investment. The main purpose of a vice is that it will hold the hook firmly. If it doesn't do this it is useless The most common types of vice use either a screw collet, or a cam lever to grip the hook. Both are very efficient, and neither one is preferred over the other. Although the very best vices can be very expensive indeed, the good news is that a perfectly serviceable vice can be had at around £30. The best advice we can offer is that you buy the best you can afford. When you buy your vice, obtain a material spring at the same time. This is a short length of spiral wire, the ends of which can be clipped together forming a ring. Slipped on to the barrel of the vice, it enables floss, ribbing and other materials to be held back out of the way whilst new materials are being tied in. Very simple and useful if you don't have three hands.

Bobbin Holder
The spigot bobbin holder is the device which holds the spool of tying thread used for tying. The tension of the arms means that the thread is only dispensed through the tube by the tension during winding. A great advantage is that the weight of the spool plus the bobbin holder is sufficient to maintain tension on the thread when it is left hanging. This means that don't have to keep securing the thread when you prepare a new material for tying in. There are two types of spigot tube, stainless steel and ceramic: both are good but the ceramic spigot is less prone to wear and tends to be slightly more expensive. At the same time as you purchase your bobbin holder, buy a threader for getting the thread through the tube.

Hackle Pliers
These come in many varied types and sizes. The main thing is that they efficiently grip the tip of a hackle or other similar delicate material without cutting it. When buying, therefore, check that they have a good sound grip, to the point where the hackle breaks before the pliers relinquish their grip, but no sharp cutting edges.

TOOLS OF THE TRADE

Dubbing Needle
The dubbing needle is more used for fine varnishing work than for picking out dubbing. Darning needles will not do for any of this work. A needle for dubbing work, picking out fibres etc. should be short and strong, with a sharp point, whereas, for varnishing the heads when finishing a fly, the needle can be longer, with a fine tapered point. It is useful therefore to have a couple of needles, one for each purpose.

Half Hitch Tool
The simplest method of finishing a fly, and no less a job at the end of it all. Comprises a barrel with a small (1.5mm dia.) hole at one end, which is slipped over the eye of the hook and the half-hitch slid onto the head. Many tyers use the end of an empty barrel of an old ball point pen, which makes a perfect half-hitch tool.

Hair Stacker
A two part tubular device for levelling the tips of hair for winging or tails.

Dubbing Twirler
The writers find this one of the most efficient ways of applying dubbing, whether it's the coarsest seal's fur or the finest mole or muskrat. It is also a brilliant tool for making hair hackles for nymphs or dry flies.

Lighting
By no means the least consideration – you must have adequate light to do the job. An Anglepoise type of lamp with a 60-100 watt bulb capacity is ideal. The 'Daylight' blue bulbs available from craft or needlework stores are superb for flytying. They are a little expensive at first, but they last a long time and the quality of light is exceptional. Avoid fluorescent light fittings as they distort colours, and are very tiring on the eyes.

Odds & Ends
Other items or implements which are very useful include:

A scalpel or small craft knife, for cutting into hide etc.

A small piece of Velcro, the barbed bit, for fluffing out dubbings, instead of using the dubbing needle.

Fine pointed tweezers for that delicate pick-up work, handy but not essential.

Fine tipped pliers, the type that jewellers might use, very useful for all sorts of work when a firm hold is required, flattening barbs or for putting a bend into a hook-shank etc.

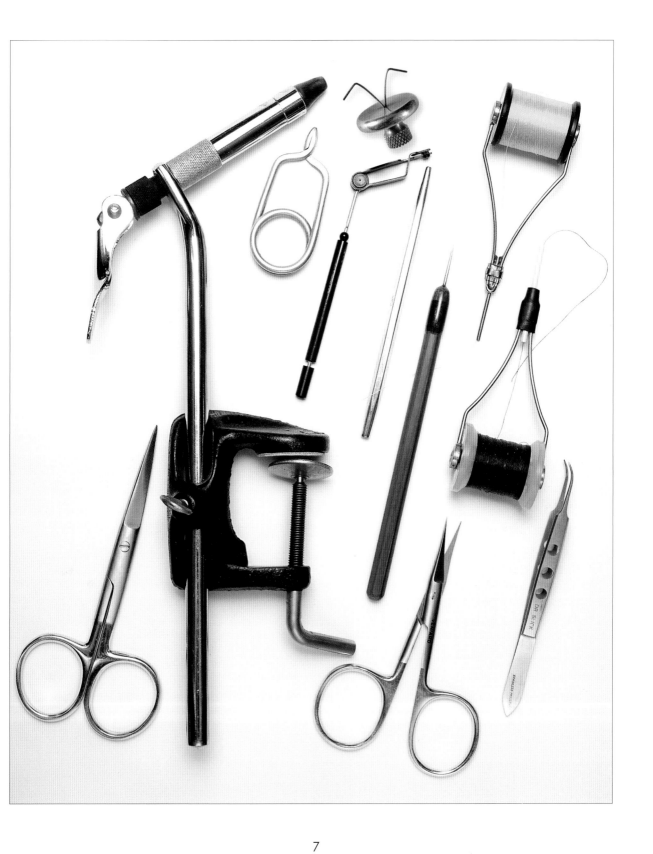

BUYING MATERIALS

As a newcomer to flytying you are actually in an enviable position. There is no other sport or hobby that we know of where a newcomer will find such a warm welcome. As flytyers we are well served by one of the few businesses in the world where the customer really does come first. Almost every retailer or mail order house is staffed by people who are keen anglers and flytyers themselves. Confronted with the bewildering array of materials that are available, the best thing you can do is ask. Explain what you want to do and almost invariably you will find that the staff are both knowledgable, helpful and unstinting in their advice. It is almost unknown for suppliers to knowingly supply bad quality or unsuitable materials – there are few other businesses in the modern world where you can say that!

BASICS

Hooks

All of the flies described in this book are tied on hooks readily available from a range of manufacturers. All of the popular brands use a chemical sharpening process so this is normally not in question. If you practice 'catch-and-release', some of the hooks are available in barbless form. Otherwise select a type with a micro-barb and crush the barb (carefully) with a pair of small pliers or forceps. Hook sizes can be confusing – a larger number means a smaller size. The size of most standard hooks are similar, even from different manufacturers. The problems start with special shapes (e.g. curved shank nymph & grub hooks). If you are not sure, refer your supplier to a standard hook – i.e. 'about the same body length as a standard size 12 wet fly hook'. Long shank hooks are measured by an X number which specifies how much longer the shank is than normal. i.e. A size 14 - 2X long means a hook which has the gape of a size 14 with the shank length of a size 10 (two sizes larger).

Threads

Most threads available today are synthetic materials which come in two basic types, twisted & un-twisted. We recommend that you use un-twisted thread as this lies flatter and grips better. Threads are graded according to thickness, the finest being 17/0, the thickest 3/0. Most trout flies are tied using either 6/0 or 8/0 thread. Pre-waxed thread is recommended, the wax dressing giving additional grip.

Floss

Most modern floss is a multi-strand untwisted yarn of synthetic fibres. Several times thicker than the thickest tying thread, it is available in a huge range of colours, including fluorescents. Some patterns call for traditional silk floss – this is a round, twisted thread which may be used as it is or untwisted.

Tinsels

There are three types of tinsel used in flytying: Flat, Oval and Round. These are available in Silver and Gold and a wide range of other colours. Many of the best are now made from synthetics, the main advantage being that they do not tarnish. In addition you will also need some Copper wire, some fine Gold wire and some lead wire for weighting.

MATERIALS & MATERIALS LIST

HAIRS & FURS

Dubbings
The most commonly-used natural dubbings are Seal's fur and Hare's fur. Others include Mole, Muskrat, Rabbit etc. Synthetics have taken over a large part of the market, and represent a large proportion of dubbings currently in use. While recipes are often specific in which dubbing to use, substitution is not out of the question. There are lots of prepared dubbing mixes available, the most useful of which are those combining natural fur with sparkle material. Some excellent seal's fur substitutes are also now available.

Bucktail
A very commonly-used hair for wings and tails. It comes in natural and a wide range of dyed colours. Look for hair that is fine and where the natural crinkle is not too exaggerated. The Grey Wulff in this book uses natural bucktail which has dark tips.

Elk Body Hair
A very good hair for wings and tails. Available as natural, bleached white and dyed. Natural with long pale golden tips is ideal for a whole range of flies. White is used on the Elk Hair Caddis to make it easier to see on the water. Note that the body hair does not flare widely when tied in. Make sure that your supplier knows that you wish to use it for wings & tails, not for spinning (hair for spinning 'flares' readily with the thread pressure and is not suitable for wings, etc).

Calf Hair
Another natural material often used for wings and tails. Slightly coarser and more crinkled than bucktail it is available in natural (brown, white) and a wide range of dyed colours. Calf hair can vary greatly in quality. Explain to your supplier that you are tying small flies as some calf tails are only suitable for large lures.

Squirrel Hair
Finer than either bucktail or calf, this hair is widely used for wings and tails. The natural tail has fibres which are dark grey to black with white tips. Squirrel tail is available in a wide range of natural colours as well as dyed colours. Normally dyed squirrel tails retain the dark barring but they can also be bleached before dying, thus producing pure colours.

Deer Hair
Deer hair is available from a wide range of species, each having its own characteristics. Most deer hair (but not all) is hollow and thus floats readily. It is therefore mainly used for wings, bodies and tails of dry and emerger flies. Because of its hollow structure, some deer hair flares widely under pressure from the tying thread. These types of hair are mainly used for 'spinning' around the hook to form buoyant heads or bodies of surface flies. The variety of these hairs is so wide that you will need to take advice from your supplier as to the most suitable for your purpose.

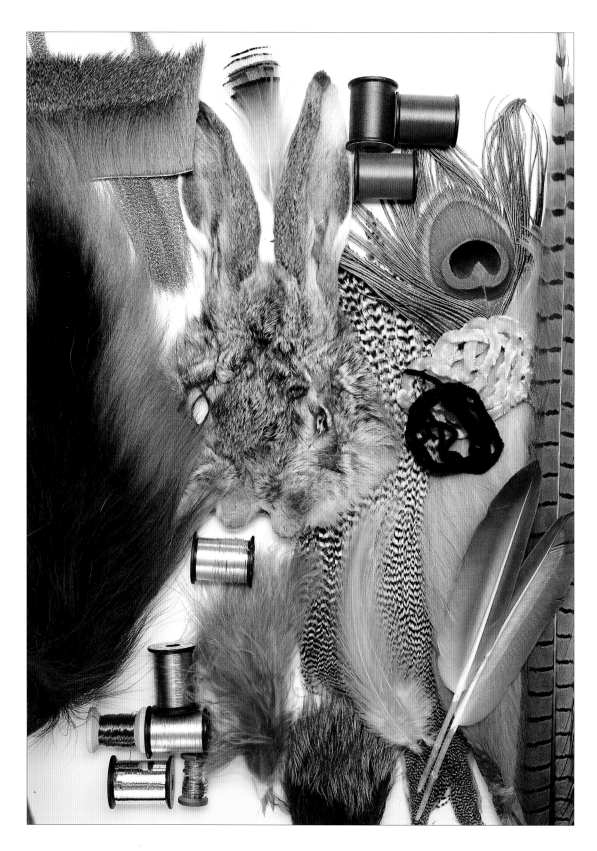

MATERIALS & MATERIALS LIST

FEATHERS

Marabou Plumes
These fluffy filoplume feathers originally came from the Marabou Stork. They are now obtained from Turkeys. Available in a vast range of colours, they are easy to obtain and cheap. Marabou is used for winging, tails and bodies on a vast range of modern flies.

Cul-de-Canard
Cul-de-Canard are naturally oiled filoplume feathers that come from around the preen gland of a duck. CDC plumes are also well endowed with barbules which trap bubbles of air, thus enhancing the floating qualities. Available in natural brown and also dyed.

Hackles
Hackles for flytying are taken from two parts of the bird's anatomy, the neck known as the Cape, which renders a wide variety of sizes of feather, and the rump known as the Saddle, which offers longer feathers. The feather fibre from the hen is soft and therefore best suited to sunk flies. The feathers from a cock bird on the other hand are altogether stiffer and give good support to a floating, or dry fly.

The most-widely used hackles are of Indian origin, they are economical, with a wide colour range. Indian capes are the smallest but nevertheless carry a good range of sizes. The Indian cock hackle is consistent in its stiffness, and the hen conversely, is nicely soft. Chinese capes are a little less reliable for hackle qualities, but they are still more than adequate for the beginner. Size of feather on the cape is the main thing to check for as they can be quite large. Some Chinese capes that are dyed can be of superb quality.

Genetic hackles come from specially bred birds and offer superb quality feathers suitable for tying dry flies down to size 18-22. They are expensive but worth the money if you need to tie lots of tiny dries. Genetic saddle capes are also particularly useful for palmered flies due to the length of the feathers offered (they can be up to 200mm - 8" long). Whilst genetic hackles are not absolutely necessary for any of the patterns in this book they would certainly be desirable for tying the Elk Hair Caddis (page 45) and the Woolly Bugger (page 73).

Feather fibre (Herl)
Apart from hackles, plumage from other parts of a bird are utilised for bodies, butts and sometimes for winging. Among the most widely-used are Ostrich herl, the tail feathers from the Common European Pheasant and the eye and sword feathers from the Peacock.

Wing Quills
Slips of fibres from wing quills are primarily used for winging flies but may also be used as herl for nymph bodies. The most useful to start with are grey duck quills as used for the Ginger Quill. Quills used for winging should always be bought in matched, opposite pairs so that identical, but opposite handed, wing slips can be obtained (see **Winging** on page 24).

OTHER MATERIALS

Chenille
This could be described as a furry rope. It is a very convenient means of making a fly body and the simplest of all to apply. Chenille comes in almost every imaginable colour, and in different sizes, from ultra fine to 'elephant', and in a wide variety of materials, from cotton through to pearlescent strand and flashy types often referred to as 'cactus'.

Crystal Hair (Krystal Hair) and other synthetics
This material is a synthetic, sparkling fibre that is often used in tails and wings to add flash to a fly. Available in a wide range of colours, the most useful are Pearl, Olive, Silver & Gold. Use sparingly for maximum effect. A huge range of other flashy, synthetic materials are also now available such as Lureflash, Twinkle, Reflections etc. each having different characteristics.

Flytyer's Wax
You will need flytyer's wax to apply to the thread when dubbing or when using a dubbing loop. Flytyer's wax comes in several forms, but the most convenient is a twist-up stick.

Varnish
Varnish comes in several types. We recommend a cellulose such as Veniard's Cellire in both clear and black. For building up larger, glossy heads, an acrylic lacquer such as Firefly Liquid Glass or Hard-as-Nails clear nail varnish is recommended.

Materials list for the flies in this book

Hooks: Medium weight down eye dry fly hooks size 10 to 16
Standard wet fly hooks size 8 to 12
Long shank lure hooks size 6 to 10
Curved lightweight grub hook size 10 to 16
Long shank nymph hook size 6 to 12
Curved heavyweight grub hook size 8 to 14
Standard nymph hooks size 6 to 12

Tying Thread: Pre waxed: 8/0 & 6/0 in Black, Brown & Medium Olive

Cock hackles: Grizzly, Olive dyed Grizzly, Medium Blue Dun, Yellow, Black, Ginger

Wing Quills: Pair of grey duck quills.

Marabou Plumes: Medium olive.

CDC Plumes: Natural brown

Chenille: Medium black & yellow

Tinsels: Medium flat & medium oval in Silver & Gold, fine oval Silver

Wires: Copper, Gold & Lead wire

Tippets: Golden Pheasant tippets

Dubbing: Fine texture muskrat, hares fur, medium olive seals fur

Herl: Cock Pheasant centre tail

Elk Hair: Natural or bleached body hair

Bucktail: Natural brown (dark tipped)

Calf Hair: Body hair white

Floss: Black

Brass Beads: 2 or 3mm diameter

Quill: Peacock eye feather

Varnish (head cement): Veniard's Cellire in clear & black. Clear Firefly Liquid Glass or Hard-As-Nails

Sparkle material: Olive Krystal hair or similar

Wax: A stick of flytyer's wax

BASIC FLYTYING TECHNIQUES

This chapter of the book explains and illustrates the basic skills of flytying. These basic skills form the building blocks on which all the more advanced techniques are based. Just as building a house successfully depends upon firm foundations, so flytying depends upon these techniques. There are no short cuts which make these steps unnecessary. The basics must be mastered before you can proceed to more advanced techniques.

Tying neat fly bodies is a typical example. If you know how to do it correctly, it is easy. If you don't, it will be nearly impossible. We understand that you are very keen to tie your first fly and to get on to your local water to try it out but please be patient – learning the basics may seem secondary to completing the first fly, but you must learn to walk before you can run. If you are prepared to invest a little time and patience in the early stages, you will be richly rewarded later. There may be a few people around who are so naturally talented that they can make it up as they go along – the rest of us need to learn and practice to master these skills. It is no accident that these techniques have been developed over hundreds of years. Many thousands of flydressers, including the masters, have found that they are the best way of doing things.

Flytying, in common with many other crafts, rewards those who make the effort to get things right from the start. It is always much easier to learn things correctly the first time, rather than to try and correct bad habits later.

There is one further point that is often overlooked – well tied flies fish better! This alone should give you the impetus that you need to work your way through these first steps. Believe us, it will pay off in the end!

BEGINNINGS & ENDINGS

Starting the Thread

Almost every flytying sequence begins with the sentence: 'Run the thread down to a point above the hook barb, in close touching turns'. The main reason for doing this is that the hook shank is slippery and the thread provides a non-slip bed on which the further materials can be tied. That explained, the question is: how do you do it?

1. Grip the hook in the vice, securing only the bend of the hook. Pull a little thread from the bobbin holder. Take the loose end in the fingers of your left hand, the bobbin holder in your right hand and holding the thread taut, place it behind the hook shank as shown in figure 1.

2. Maintaining the tension on the thread, use the bobbin holder end to wind the thread once around the hook shank, ending up at the bottom again.

3. Now take another 2 or 3 turns back towards the hook bend, so that the thread is securely trapped, holding the tension so that the thread does not slip.

4. Now continue to take further turns, back towards the hook bend. If you keep the loose end of the thread held tautly at an angle and place each turn a little way up the slope, it will slide down as it is tightened, butting up snugly against its neighbour.

Whip Finishing

Whip finishing is the best way of securing the thread when you have finished tying the fly. Basically it involves threading the loose end of the thread back under the last four or five turns of thread taken around the hook shank. What we actually do is to hold the loose end of the thread parallel to the hook shank whilst we take the last four or five turns over this. The loose end is then pulled tight. The detail in Figure 4 opposite, shows what we want to achieve. This procedure is actually far more difficult to describe than to do.

1. Take a loop of thread and insert your fore- and second finger as shown in figure 1, holding tension on the loose end of the thread with your left hand.

2. Tuck the part of the thread that runs parallel to the hook shank under the thread that goes round the hook, using your second finger to hold the thread in position.

3. Now take a turn of thread around the shank, using the open part of the loop. Do this by revolving your index finger around the hook shank, keeping the loop under tension. Your second finger should stay in front of the hook.

4. As your fingers come up the front of the hook, you must reverse their positions inside the loop so that the second finger again pulls the parallel part of the thread down into the correct position. The most important thing is that the parallel part of the thread must not go around the shank.

5. Repeat this procedure another four times and then finally, holding the open part of the loop tight, draw the loose end slowly through, closing the loop until it snugs tight up against the previous turns. Trim off the waste end of the thread and the fly is finished.

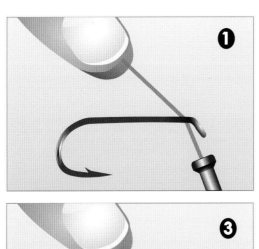

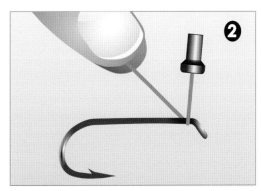

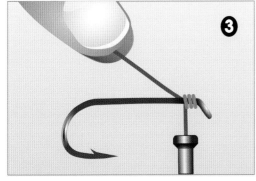

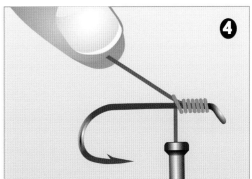

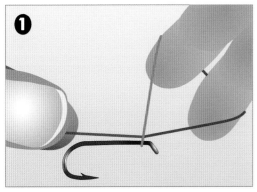

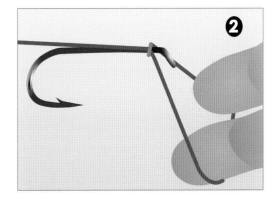

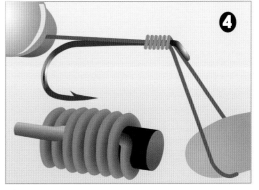

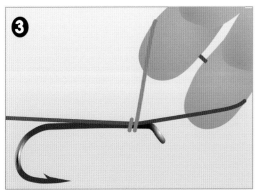

BASIC FLYTYING TECHNIQUES

GENERAL PRINCIPLES

The hook and tying thread

At the beginning you will find that it is all too easy to break the tying thread. This is due mainly to two reasons. Firstly, applying too much pressure to the thread; it takes some time to acquire a feel for the correct amount. A very useful exercise which we strongly recommend, is to put a strong hook in the vice and after securing the tying thread, really apply tension to the thread until it breaks. This is the quickest and easiest way to get a 'feel' for how much tension you can apply to a thread.

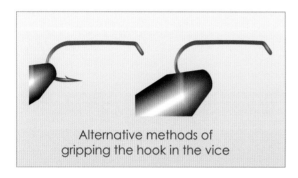

Alternative methods of
gripping the hook in the vice

Secondly, if you are not careful, the thread can often be cut by the protruding point of the hook in the vice. Throughout this book we have shown the hook held in the vice only by the bend. This is preferred by most experienced tyers as it avoids the chance of weakening the point of the hook. There is however no need to be a martyr to this. If you find that it causes a problem or if you catch your fingers on the barb, then set the hook in the vice so as to cover the point.

The art of gentle persuasion

Another of the common causes of problems is the tendency to try and 'make' the materials take the correct position. Gentle persuasion is the order of the day here – materials should be manoeuvred into position, not forced.

An understanding of the mechanics of securing materials by winding turns of thread over them is important. It should be obvious that as you wind the thread over the materials and the hook shank, there is a natural tendency for the materials to be dragged with the thread and forced over the shank. The tighter the tension on the thread, the more pronounced this will be. One way of overcoming this problem is to try and hold the materials in position against the force of the thread. This may work sometimes but it is much better to throw a **loose** turn of thread over the hook and only apply the tension when the thread is hanging vertically downwards. This can be extended further by using the '**pinch & loop**' method shown on page 25. This will minimise the dragging and only light pressure will be needed to hold the material in position, causing the minimum of distortion. Work **with** the materials, don't fight **against** them.

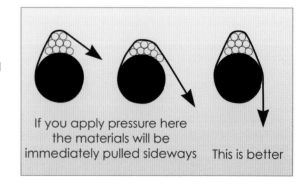

If you apply pressure here
the materials will be
immediately pulled sideways   This is better

BASIC FLYTYING TECHNIQUES

BODIES

The first requisite is that the underbody windings of thread need to be smoothly tapered and free of lumps and bumps. One of the main caused of unevenness in the underbody is the cutting off short of other tying materials such as tail fibres and ribbing. We recommend that these ends should be left as long as the fly body and then bound down with a smooth layer of tying thread. In this way lumps will be avoided. Another common cause of lumps in the body is the use of too many turns of tying thread at the tail position where as many as four components need to be tied in. Two or three turns are sufficient for most materials.

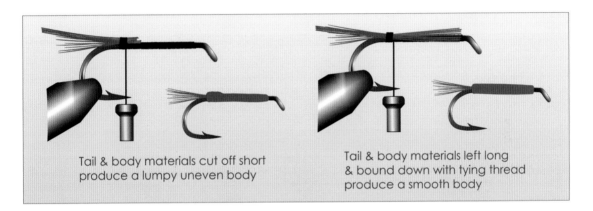

Tail & body materials cut off short
produce a lumpy uneven body

Tail & body materials left long
& bound down with tying thread
produce a smooth body

Floss bodies

The idea with a floss body is that it should look smooth and silky. Handling floss is a delicate business, and any nicks in your fingertips will cause problems. We suggest that you avoid this problem by gripping the loose end in a pair of hackle pliers, and use it that way. The procedure is quite simple. Tie the floss in near the eye at the front of the body, wind it back towards the bend, then back towards the eye, untwisting as you progress in order that the floss lies flat. Each time you wind the floss around the body, the fibres of the floss rotate through 180 degrees and will become tightly twisted. To taper the body, overlap the turns more where you want it to be fatter. If you are using your fingers, don't let go of the floss when you are winding. If you do, it will unravel into a fluffy mess.

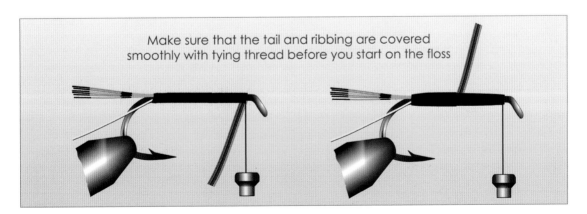

Make sure that the tail and ribbing are covered
smoothly with tying thread before you start on the floss

Herl bodies

A small bunch of maybe three or four or more fibres are used to create the body or thorax of a fly. When winding herl bodies, you will sometimes see a recommendation that two or more strands should be twisted together to add strength. We disagree strongly with this approach. Twisting the herls reduces them to a lifeless, lumpy rope. The increase in strength will be minimal and is far better achieved by using a fine wire ribbing after the herl is wound. Another alternative is to coat the underbody with varnish and allow this to go tacky before winding the herl. When winding the rope of fibres, ensure that the turns do not overlap as this will produce unsightly lumps.

Quill bodies

This is a body formed our of a single feather stalk, often from the eye feather of the peacock but it may come from other sources. Before winding, the quill should be stripped of its herl. The turns should abut one another and not overlap. Make sure that the quill is not twisted as it is wound. Be gentle when winding – stripped quill can be delicate!

Tinsel bodies

There are many occasions when tinsel is used to form the fly body itself. To achieve a smooth body, it is best to tie the flat tinsel in at the front of the body, winding it back towards the tail, and then forwards again to the start position. The underbody which is formed by the turns of tying thread is of critical importance for the formation of a tinsel body. Any bumps and unevenness in the underbody will be exaggerated and made worse when the tinsel is wound. Keep an even tension when winding.

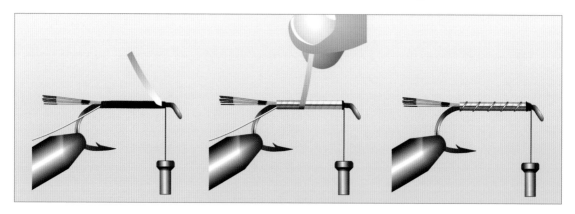

Smooth bodies are easier to produce with narrower tinsel – wide metallic tinsel which is quite thick and strong is the most difficult to use. With wide tinsel, cut off the end at an angle before tying in – take two turns of thread to secure, fold the sharp end back on itself and secure with another couple of turns of thread. When using wide tinsels, the turns should be overlapped by a small amount, the tinsel being held under quite strong pressure so that the turns 'bed down'. Tips about making tinsel bodies more robust can be found under **Tough Tinsel** on page 52.

Dubbing bodies

This is a means of applying loose fur or other fibre to the hook to form a body or thorax. The most common method is to twist it directly onto the thread. We have assumed that you are using pre-waxed thread but you may find that an extra application of flytying wax to the thread will help a lot here. Take a **small amount** of dubbing and tease it out so that the fibres are loosened. Using the thumb and forefinger, twist the fibres along the tying thread to form a loose spindle. This can be helped by also twisting the thread in the same direction. The most common fault is to try and use too much dubbing – too little is always better than too much. Wind the dubbing rope forward in even turns without overlapping the wraps.

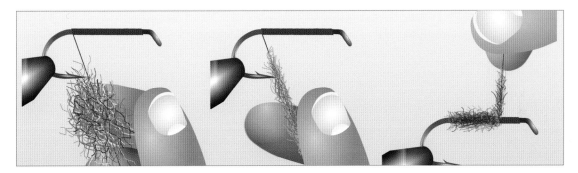

The dubbing loop

The method shown above is suitable for most bodies but there are occasions when it will not be the easiest. When you wish to use a coarse material that will not readily wind round the thread or when you wish to use extra long fibres to produce a leggy effect, the best method is to use a dubbing loop and twirler as explained on page 48, **The Dubbing Loop**.

Ribbing

The ribbing material should be tied in underneath the shank, rather than on top. With oval tinsel you can strip back the metallic coating to expose the core and tie this in. Otherwise, leave the ends as long as the body and bind down with turns of thread as explained on page 17. This will avoid lumps at the tying-in position. Ribbing should be as evenly spaced as possible – this sounds easy, but is more difficult than it seems. Keep the ribbing tight and under an even tension when winding. About five turns of ribbing is usual for a standard length hook; more may be better for a long shank hook.

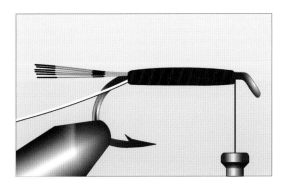
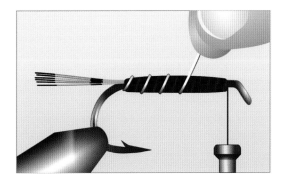

Tails

There are two ways to ensure that the tail sits correctly on top of the shank. You can offer the fibres to the front of the shank, at an angle of about 30 degrees, and let the turns of thread draw the fibres onto the top of the hook. Even better, you can use a **loose** turn of thread and only tighten with a vertical pull after the thread has been brought round to the front of the shank (see page 25, **Pinch & Loop**).

HACKLING

There are a number of ways of applying the hackle to your fly. The styles you will need are commonly named as follows: Collar, Palmered, Beard, Throat and Parachute. All of these styles are dealt with in greater detail below. Further tips on hackling are also to be found on page 60, **Hackling Hints**.

Collar hackle

A hackle can be tied-in either by its butt, or by its tip, giving very different effects. The butt method is usually used with conventional dry flies whereas the tip method is better for wet patterns. By tying the butt first, the hackle will sit upright, whereas if it is tied by the tip it will 'sweep' better. The reason for this is that the stalk of a feather has a pronounced taper. If the butt is tied-in first, subsequent wraps are supported by a thick stalk; conversely, the tip method has the opposite effect (there is little support from a thinner stalk at the rear of each turn, so the hackle sits back more readily). The fibre lengths also play a role here if the hackle is tied in butt-first, the first turns will have the longest fibres, subsequent turns being shorter. If the tip is tied in first, the opposite is true – the first turns are shorter, subsequent turns produce longer fibres which will sweep back over the previous turns more easily.

Wet Fly Style
Hackle tied-in by tip
Hackle doubled and
swept backwards

Dry Fly Style
Hackle tied-in by stalk
Hackle sits upright
Hackle not doubled

Whichever method is used, all the fluffy fibres around the base of the stalk should be stripped away and the hackle tied in using several tight turns of thread. Once it is secure the hackle pliers should then clipped to the other end so that winding can begin. The wide 'ring' in the hackle pliers is provided so that you can use your finger to wind under tension without the hackle twisting. Successive turns of hackle should be made, one in front of another towards the head of the fly. The hackle is then be secured with several tight turns of thread. The pliers can now be removed and the excess hackle clipped away.

Doubled collar hackle

In appearance, the wet collar hackle is usually swept backwards towards the tail. This effect is aided if the hackle is tied in by the tip, rather than by the stalk.

To help this effect, the hackle can be 'doubled'. Doubling means that the hackle should be folded back on itself into a vee-form with the best side of the fibres lying on the outside of the vee. The doubling may be done before the hackle is tied in or it may be done during the winding by stroking and holding the fibres backwards between the thumb and forefinger, as the wraps proceed. You may find that moistening the fingers helps here. A doubled hackle presents a denser appearance than a conventionally wound hackle and therefore needs fewer turns.

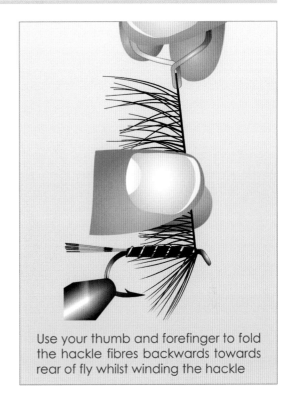

Use your thumb and forefinger to fold the hackle fibres backwards towards rear of fly whilst winding the hackle

The Palmered hackle

This is a hackle which runs the length of the body of a fly in spiral turns and has been a popular device ever since a fly was offered to trout. The hackle is normally tied in at the head of the fly by the butt, and wrapped rearwards so that the fibres decrease in length towards the rear of the fly. It is secured by turns of a wire rib brought forward in the opposite spiral trapping the hackle stalk at every turn. A bit of judicious wiggling about of the ribbing during this procedure may be necessary to avoid trapping the hackle fibres, use a dubbing needle to nudge the fibres out of the way if necessary. A palmered hackle should not be too closely wrapped, open turns are far better in fishing terms. Dry fly palmers are normally more closely wrapped than sub-surface patterns.

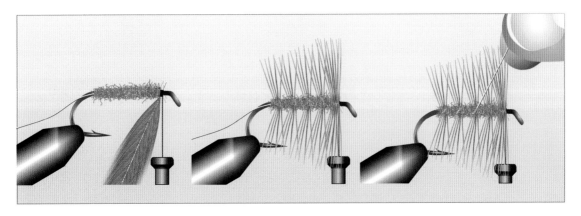

BASIC FLYTYING TECHNIQUES

BEARD & THROAT HACKLES

These two terms are often used interchangeably but strictly speaking they should be used as explained below. The throat hackle gives a much fuller, more widely spread appearance and lies at a greater angle to the body.

The Beard hackle

Basically a beard hackle is a bunch of hackle fibres which is tied in under the head of the fly directly behind the eye. It may help to invert the hook in the vice, but if you can avoid this then so much the better. Offer the fibres up to the hook and take two positioning turns of thread. If you want to spread these fibres, roll your thumbnail over the turns – the fibres will 'flare'. This can be done with precision, the flaring being controlled to just the desired amount. Finish off with two or three securing turns and then trim away the waste.

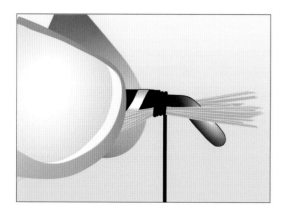 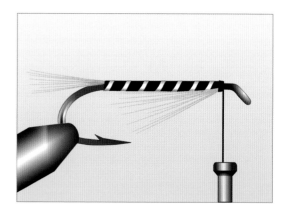

The Throat hackle

A throat hackle is initially applied as a full wrap around the hook, and then manipulated with the fingers and secured so that it ends up sitting only on the underside of the fly. The hackle is first tied in as a normal collar hackle. The fibres that sit above the hook shank are then pulled down with the thumb and forefinger to the underside of the hook and held in position. A couple of turns of tying thread are applied at a slight angle across the roots to hold them in place.

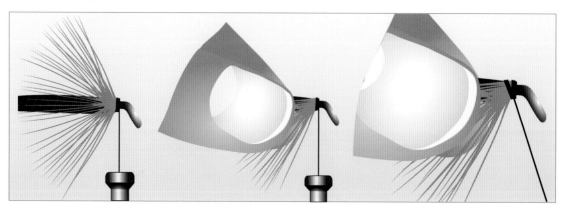

The Parachute hackle

A parachute hackle is wound round a near vertical 'wing' and thus produces a hackle which is substantially parallel to the hook shank. Because it has to be wound tightly around the wing, it is important to select a hackle which has a thin, flexible stalk. The more rigid the base is, the easier it will be to wind the hackle around it. For this reason a bed of tying thread is first wound around the bottom of the wing to produce a more stable base. The judicious use of a couple of drops of varnish at the base can also be of great assistance. A special tool called the **gallows tool** is also available which can be fixed to the vice and is used to hold the top end of the wing during the winding process. The winding of the hackle should proceed in a downwards direction – i.e. the first turn is at the top; all succeeding turns are made below in a spiral fashion.

In the graphic below the hackle stalk has been coloured white to show the spiral winding from top to bottom. The windings are greatly exaggerated for clarity.

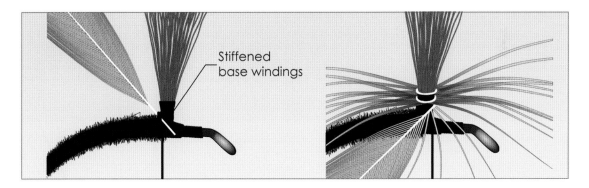

Stiffened base windings

The final tying off of a parachute hackle can be a problem but the following method makes it simple. Hold the hackle tip towards you, together with the tying thread, and twist them together two or three times as a sort of loose rope. Now make two turns more of this rope around the base of the wing and then release and trim away the hackle tip. The wrapping of a parachute hackle will often throw out stray fibres, which don't sit precisely where you want them. If they sit below the base line of the body, just trim them away, it's not a crime.

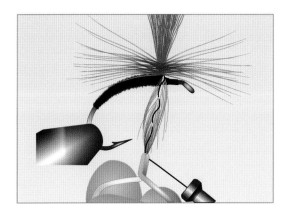
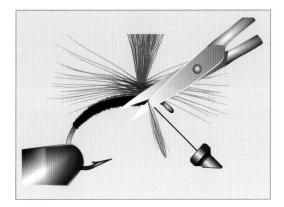

WINGING

Winging is often considered to be the most difficult part of flytying. There is however no great mystique or trickery, just a couple of basic principles to bear in mind. These two principles can be summarized thus: know your material and use its natural characteristics to help you achieve what you want.

Feather slip wings

When you are working with feather fibre, you have to understand the natural attributes of the material. Each fibre of a quill feather is connected to its neighbour by a series of 'hooks and eyes'. This arrangement keeps the feather together in flight and will also keep it together during tying – if you let it! If you fold or pull the fibres sideways, the hold will fail and the slip will disintegrate, no matter how tightly you hold the feathers.

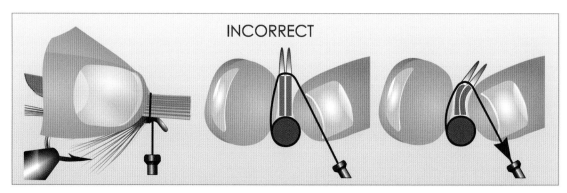

INCORRECT

The first steps to ensure a good wing are taken even before we start to tie the feathers in. This begins with taking a matched pair of slips from the same position on opposing feathers. It is important that both slips are the same width. If they are not, an even compression is impossible. The best way to ensure this is to use a dubbing needle to separate out the slip and to count the number of fibres. The width of the slips should be between 3/16 and 1/3 of the finished wing length i.e. from 2.5 to 4mm for a 12mm wing (see **Proportions** on page 40). Secondly, it will help a great deal if you can pull the fibres away from the stalk with your fingers, retaining a bit of quill, rather than cutting them out with scissors. Thirdly, the length of the slips should match the length of the wings required. If you select very long slips and tie them in near the tips, the natural curve of the feather is lost and the number of 'hooks & eyes' will be less, making it more difficult to keep the slips together.

There is a natural curve to the slips. Usually they are tied in like this

but they could be tied in this way round

BASIC FLYTYING TECHNIQUES

Pinch & loop

With the pinch & loop method we avoid the wing fibres rolling and separating by applying the tension only when the thread is vertical. Because the thread passes between our fingers instead of in front of them, we can also hold the fibres in position across the complete area that is affected by the tying-in process. This technique can also be used for a variety of other purposes, such as tying in tails, where it is important that the fibres are not dragged round the hook shank.

STEP 1

First make sure you have a flat bed of thread to mount the wings on to. Carefully match the two slips together dull-side-to-dull-side/concave-to-concave and, gripping them between the thumb and forefinger, offer them up to the top of the hook, positioning them exactly in line with the shank. You will find that with a bit of practice, the bottom part of your finger and thumb will hold the hook, bringing everything in line. The wing should extend at least to the bend of the hook (see **Proportions** on page 40).

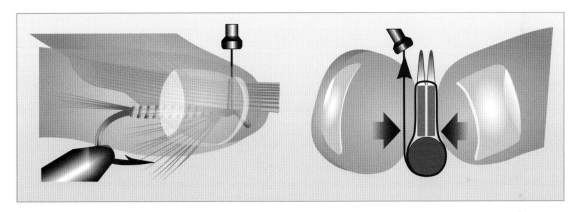

STEP 2

Once the wing length is established, take a loose turn of thread up over the wing and passing down the other side, **between your fingers and the hook**, without any tension on the top of wing segment. The 'pinch' between the thumb and forefingers should be loose enough so as to allow the thread to pass between. A little gentle jockeying may be necessary here.

STEP 3

Now bring the thread up at the front, again **between the two fingers and the hook**. When you have done this, tension can then be applied to the thread in an upward direction. Keep your grip firm whilst doing this, but not too tight. With the tension being applied in a vertical direction, the feather fibres will compress tidily, one on top of another.

You can now remove your fingers and take a look to see if the wing is set correctly. If it is, make a few turns, but no more than half a dozen, in front of the other turns to secure it. Trim off the waste ends of the wing butts as closely as possible and finish off with neat turns of thread.

Hair wings

The main problem with hair wings is making sure that the hair is tied in securely, and that it stays tied in when fishing. One of the main reasons for hair coming loose, is to attempt to tie in too large a bunch in one go. If you err, err on the side of too little hair.

Most natural hair has a thick, fine underfur between the longer hairs. If you try to tie in a bunch of hair without removing the underfur you will have problems as the wing will not be secure once these shorter hairs start to come loose. Step number one, therefore: clean out all the underfur, leaving only the longer guard hairs.

The tips of the hair can be evened up in two ways. If you want a tapered, graduated look you can do this by hand; otherwise you can use a hair stacker which will produce a more even effect. Full details of this procedure can be found in **Tricks of the Trade 9 – Hair Raising Stuff** on page 64.

Offer up the wing on top of the hookshank. Take a couple of turns to hold the wing in position and check the length. Take another two tight turns to the right of the first turns. leaving a gap between. Now move back between these two wrappings and take one more tight turn between them – the idea is to form a series of crimps in the hair.

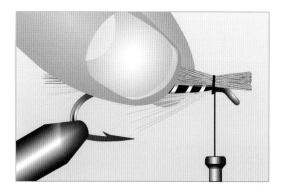
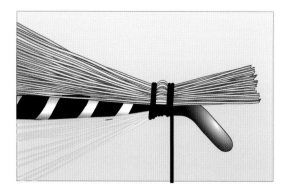

Now lift the wing and take one or two turns around the base of the wing fibres so that they stay together as a bunch. Take a few more turns in front and then trim away the waste hair at an angle just in front of the eye. A drop or two of varnish on the windings will help to keep everything secure. But be careful, don't let it run back into the wing itself.

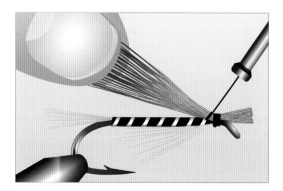
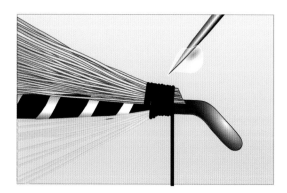

TWELVE FLY PATTERNS

This chapter of the book gives you the step-by-step dressing instructions for twelve flies. Each of these flies have been carefully chosen to illustrate a different aspect of flytying.

The flies chosen have been selected for three reasons:

1. They each demonstrate and use one or more of the techniques that you will have seen in the previous chapter.

2. They represent a range of fly types – nymphs, lures, wet flies, emergers and dry flies.

3. They are very successful fishing flies for a whole range of conditions and circumstances on various water types throughout the year.

As you will note from these patterns, many of the most effective fishing flies are not difficult to tie, indeed there is a very good case for saying that simplicity is one of the most important factors in the development of successful new patterns. Each of these patterns in its own way, features particular 'trigger factors' which can prove irresistible to the trout.

This trigger factor varies with the type of pattern – The Duck's Dun, for example, has a silhouette which exactly mimics the natural fly and it sits in the water in the correct position (this is most important – even if the fly looks right, it will not attract trout if it sits in the wrong attitude). The Woolly Bugger attracts trout, not by being an exact imitation, but rather by mimicking the sinuous swimming movement of certain nymphs in an exaggerated manner. The Shrimp is a close imitation of a natural food item, much loved by trout. The TG Parachute Emerger combines a good imitation of the natural fly with the correct and typical emergent attitude in the water. The Black Ghost lure attracts trout by a combination of colour and movement which trigger an aggressive reaction in the trout. The Goldhead Hare's Ear is an impressionistic imitation of a whole range of edible items. The weight provided by the gold head also produces a sinuous movement in the water which trout find very attractive.

For each of the patterns, we have listed the materials required, together with suggested hook types and sizes. If there is something particularly interesting about the materials used, we have given further information about its most important features. For other flies we have suggested further patterns which share the major characteristics of the detailed pattern. These further patterns are tied in a very similar manner to the pattern which is shown and are useful additional flies that you may wish to attempt.

Now a couple of points about the step-by-step instructions. The sequences use techniques which are explained in detail in the **Basic Flytying Techniques** section in Chapter 2. We recommend that you read through the instructions fully before starting to tie a new fly. In this way you can refer back to the detailed instructions, to refresh your memory as to the correct procedures, before you start.

In the illustrations, in order to make the tying steps clearer, certain things are purposely not drawn to scale. This does not concern the flies themselves, which are always drawn in the correct proportions, but may apply to other objects such as hackle pliers etc. These may have been reduced in size for example, in order that they do not obscure the detail that we wish to show.

Finally, we recommend that you follow the instructions and do not try to cut corners. There is always a temptation to do this when the reasons for a particular procedure are not immediately clear – laying down an even bed of tying thread is a typical case. In our instructions, however, there is always a good reason why a certain step is done – you may find, for example, that without the even bed of tying thread, it becomes extremely difficult to get a wing or tail to stay in the correct position

BLACK PENNELL – a classic hackled wet fly

MATERIALS

HOOK: Standard wet fly size 8-16

THREAD: Black 6/0

TAIL: GP tippet fibres

RIB: Fine oval silver tinsel

BODY: Black floss

HACKLE: Dyed black cock hackle

The Black Pennell was devised in Scotland at about the turn of the 19th Century by Mr. H. C. Cholmondley-Pennell (a real Victorian name if ever there was one, pronounced 'Chumley'). If the name of its inventor is a bit high-falutin, the fly itself is as simple as can be. Do not be deceived by this simplicity. This is one of the all-time great flies which can be found in fly boxes in every country in the world where fishing for trout takes place. Its inventor carried a range of these flies, tied in different colours, most of which are no longer in use, although the claret version can still be found in Scotland. The Black Pennell is equally effective for wild brown trout and rainbow trout and, tied in larger sizes, sometimes with the addition of a palmered body hackle, is also a very effective pattern for sea trout and salmon. It is no wonder that it has stood the test of time.

The Black Pennell is a very good imitation of a hatching buzzer (chironomid), a good imitation of many other dark flies and a fair imitation of a beetle, an ant or just about anything else which is dark coloured and good to eat (from the trout's point of view).

Although it will take fish throughout the year, the Black Pennell is probably at its best early in the season when black midge are hatching.

Like the Montana Nymph, the inventor of the Black Pennell did an invaluable service not only to fly fishermen, but particularly to flytyers. Tying the Black Pennell is simple, the materials are cheap and easy to come by and the details are not critical.

In certain parts of Scotland the Pennell is tied with an extremely short body (as little as two or three turns of floss), using a long soft hen hackle rather than a cock hackle. In this form the Pennell is a typical 'spider' and, fished under the surface, represents the nymphal form of many flies. It is certainly effective. Another variant has a very slim body and a hackle which is reduced to a single turn – it is called, appropriately, the 'Anorexic Pennell'. Another interesting variant, tied with a shorter body and a Greenwell hackle instead of black (see left), is also well worth trying.

BLACK PENNELL – a classic hackled wet fly

Step-by-Step Tying Instructions

STEP 1

Set the hook in the vice, taking hold only of the bend of the hook. From a position about 2-3mm (1/8") from the eye, run the thread back to a point above the barb, in close touching turns.

STEP 2

Now set the Golden Pheasant tippet tails. Use about 4 to 8 fibres depending upon hook size. The length of the tail from the tying in position should be about ¾ of the hook shank length. You may find it easier to 'lift' the tail fibres into position by offering them up to the hook shank on your side of the hook and letting the pressure of the tying thread bring them up to the top. Use 2 or 3 turns of thread to secure.

STEP 3

Now the ribbing tinsel can be tied in. Strip off some of the outer metallic coating for about 3mm (1/8") to expose the core and catch it in at the bottom of the hook shank in the same position as where the tail is tied in.

STEP 4

Now wind the tying thread forward, back to the position near the eye where you started, tying down the tail fibres as you go. Tie in a length of black floss.

STEP 5

Wind the floss backwards towards the bend of the hook in even turns, untwisting it as you do so, so that the fibres tend to open out. If you do this you will find it easier to produce a flat evenly tapered body. If you are using an untwisted multi-strand floss this process is easier, providing that you do not twist it when you are winding it. When you reach the tying in point of the tail, reverse direction and wind the floss back to the starting position.

Ideally you are trying to produce an even, cigar-shaped body. This process may take some practice before you become proficient. Tie off the floss and cut away the excess.

STEP 6

Now take the tinsel between forefinger and thumb and wind it towards the head in evenly spaced turns trying to keep an even tension on the ribbing as you are winding it. About 5 or 6 turns of the ribbing is about right. Try to arrange it so that the tinsel is tied off at the underside of the hook. Trap the end with 2 or 3 turns of thread and cut away the waste,

STEP 7

Select a black cock hackle with a fibre length approximately 1½ times as long as the hook gape. Remove the flue at the base end to expose the bare stalk. You will see that the hackle is not identical on both sides; one side will be shinier than the other (called the 'best' side). Tie in the hackle so that the shiny side faces towards the head of the fly. After securing the stem with 3 or 4 turns of thread, cut off the waste end. Grip the hackle tip in the hackle pliers and, without twisting it, wind on 2 or 3 turns, each turn in front of the last. Secure the hackle stalk with 2 or 3 turns of thread, and carefully, trim away the waste with your scissors. This procedure is fully explained in the section Hackling on page 20.

STEP 8

Finish the fly with several turns of thread, making a small neat head – do not overdo this. Make secure by either whipping or take a couple of half-hitches. Complete the head with a drop or two of varnish – do not use too much so that it runs into the hackle.

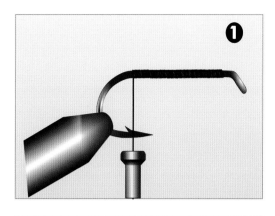

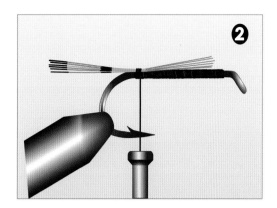

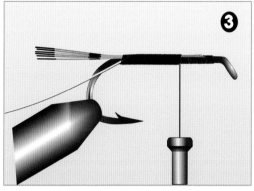

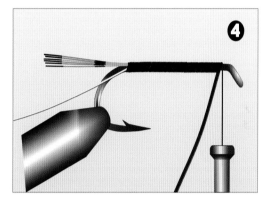

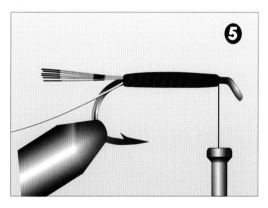

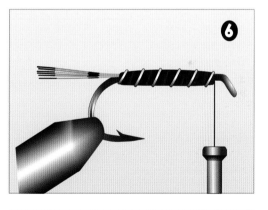

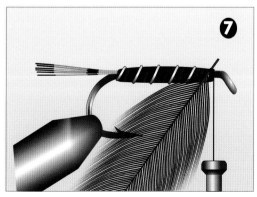

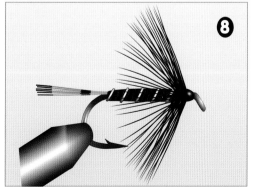

TRICKS OF THE TRADE 1: GETTING ORGANISED

To tie flies successfully you need to be properly organised. If you are not sitting comfortably, if you cannot see properly, and if you do not have your tools readily to hand, you cannot expect to produce quality work.

The room where you work needs to have good natural light. Ideally you should place your working table so that light from the window falls from the left, or from the right, rather than from in front or behind.

Your working table should have a mat or underlay on it, preferably white. A piece of stout card is ideal and can be replaced when necessary. You will be amazed how difficult it can be to spot a small hook or brown feather on a normal wooden top. A word of warning here – don't clamp your vice on to the table without some packing so as to avoid scratching the surface. Serious trouble can be expected if you ignore this!

At night (or even during daylight), you will need additional lighting on your working bench. A table light with an adjustable head and arm is ideal. The light should accept a bulb of 60 to 100 Watts. Normal light bulbs and most fluorescent tubes distort colours so badly, that it becomes impossible to see what a colour really looks like. This can lead to a shock the next morning, when the medium olive dubbing that you thought you had mixed, turns out to be bright green! Most craft shops as well as suppliers of tying materials can supply 'daylight' bulbs which are colour-corrected to be very close to natural light. They cost a bit more but are well worth it and last quite a long time. Set the lamp, behind and to the left of your vice.

It is not always possible, but if you can arrange things so that the wall or background behind your tying table is of a light, plain colour, you will also find this advantageous. If this isn't possible, another large sheet of white card can help.

Fit yourself up with some kind of 'tidy' – a plastic bag mounted on a wire frame is ideal. Into this bag, which can be clamped on the table near to hand, go all the offcuts, waste, feather fluff etc. which you will generate in quantities that you would not believe possible.

Set out your tools in some kind of holder so that they are always to hand. A simple block of polystyrene with some holes in it is sufficient if your budget does not stretch to anything more elaborate. Tools always fall on the floor, especially dubbing needles, so a retaining strip of some kind along the front of the table is very useful.

Make sure that the floor is clear of obstructions around your table and ideally have some kind of rubber mat to cover the general area. Small hooks are almost impossible to find on dark-coloured carpets and if they are not retrieved can cause serious damage to other household members, both human and animal.

MONTANA – a modern nymph

MATERIALS

HOOK: Long shank nymph hook size 6-12

THREAD: Black 6/0

WEIGHT: Optional – 0.4mm (0.015")
diameter lead wire

ABDOMEN: Black chenille

WING CASE: Black chenille

THORAX: Yellow chenille

HACKLE: Dyed black cock hackle

The Montana Nymph was first tied by Lew Oatman of New York as an imitation of an American stonefly nymph. The stonefly is essentially a creature of fast flowing, freestone rivers and judging by the name, Lew Oatman had the rivers of Montana in mind when he named the fly. The fact that it was originally conceived as a river pattern has not stopped the Montana proving to be effective in many other circumstances.

Since its conception the Montana has spread throughout the world and has become one of the classic nymph patterns. In the United Kingdom it is best known as a highly successful nymph pattern on stillwaters and lakes that have never seen a stonefly.

The Montana can be tied in both weighted and unweighted forms and is an ideal fly for the newcomer to flytying. It is easy to tie, it uses materials that are cheap and easy to obtain and is a fly which has proved its effectiveness in a wide range of fishing circumstances. There are few other flies which combine these advantages so happily.

Modern stillwater tyings have tended to replace the yellow colour of the thorax with fluorescent yellow and green. Variants with hot and fluorescent orange also exist. There is however no doubt that the use of black and yellow as used in the original is a killing combination, especially for rainbow trout. Some tyings of the original pattern also have a red, rather than black, head.

Variants which are also worth trying:
Replace the yellow thorax with fluorescent chenille – most commonly used are yellow, green and orange.

Replace the black thread for the head with fluorescent red or yellow floss.

MONTANA – a modern nymph

Step-by-Step Tying Instructions

STEP 1

Set the hook in the vice, taking hold only of the bend of the hook. From a position about 2-3mm (1/8") from the eye, run the thread back to a point above the barb, in close touching turns. If a weighted version of the fly is required, bring the thread back to the front position and tie in a length of 0.4mm (0.015") diameter, round lead wire. Wind the thread back to the rear position, followed by the lead wire in close turns. Tie off with a few turns of thread and remove the waste material.

STEP 2

Now catch in three black hackle tips for the tail. They should extend about 2/3rds of the hook length from the tying in point and should lie on the top of the hook shank. Don't cut off the waste ends at this stage as this will make a step in the body. The waste ends will be tied down when we wind the thread forward. Ideally these hackle tips should be spread out fan-wise but if you can't manage this, don't worry, it is not vitally important.

STEP 3

Tie in a length of black chenille. To prepare the chenille, strip away the outer flue coating for about 3mm (1/8") to expose the core. Tie in using only the core and then bring the thread forward in close turns to a position about 2/3rds of the way along the shank.

STEP 4

Wind the chenille forwards in close turns to the same point as the thread and secure with two turns at the top of the hook shank. Do not cut off the excess material. At the same position tie in the tip of the black cock hackle.

The hackle fibre length should be a little longer than the gape of the hook and the feather should be prepared by stripping away the flue from the base of the stalk. Full instructions on this procedure are given in **Hackling** on page 20. The hackle is then followed by a length of yellow chenille secured in the same manner as the black chenille.

STEP 5

Bring the tying thread forward to the starting position near the eye and then wind the yellow chenille forward in touching turns. Tie off with two turns of thread and cut away the waste.

STEP 6

Now take the tip of the black hackle in the hackle pliers and wind it forwards in open turns over the yellow chenille. About three turns will be correct. When you reach the front, secure the hackle with another two turns of thread and cut away the waste.

STEP 7

Take hold of the black chenille – remember, the one you didn't trim off before, and lay it across the top of the yellow thorax. This will part and flatten the hackle fibres that are pointing upwards. Stretch the chenille forwards and at the eye position take several turns of thread to fasten it and then cut away the waste.

STEP 8

Build up a small neat head of tying thread, whip finish and apply some varnish to finish off.

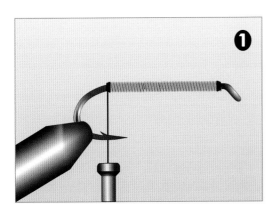

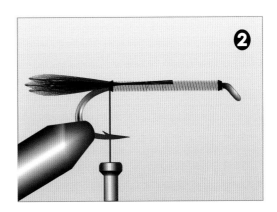

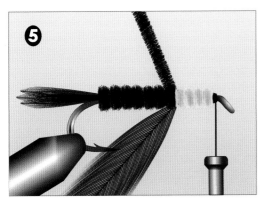

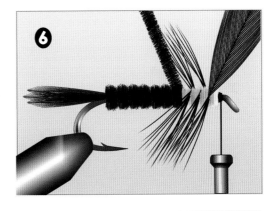

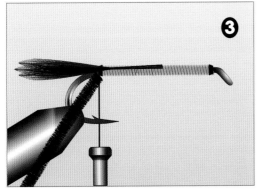

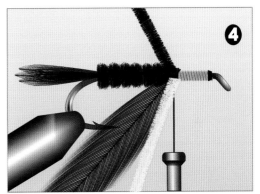

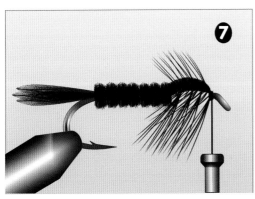

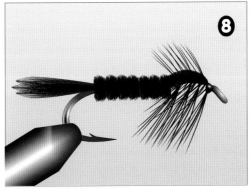

The following diagrams and notes will help you to establish positions on the hook when starting to tie a fly. In the dressing instructions you will find references to two very important positions as shown on the diagram below:

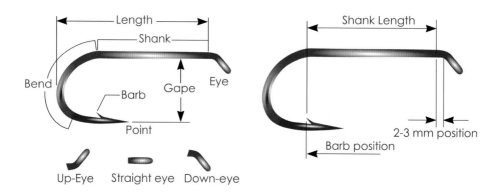

The 2-3mm Position:
This is a point approximately 2-3mm (l/8") behind the eye of the hook. This distance is required to avoid the dressing encroaching on to the eye and to provide room for you to finish off the head. Obscuring the eye is often a problem for the beginner (and is not unknown with tyers of many years experience). The 2-3mm measurement should not be regarded as fixed – it is rather intended as a guide. The distance will vary depending upon the size of the hook and the amount of material to be tied in.

Note that if you are tying in throat, beard or collar hackles in addition to a wing, you will need to leave more room, otherwise the windings for the wing will overlap those for the hackle and flatten it down.

The Barb Position:
This is a position on the hook shank, vertically above the hook barb. It may coincide with the start of the bend, but not always.

BLACK GHOST – a hairwing lure

MATERIALS

HOOK: Long shank lure hook size 6-10

THREAD: Black 6/0

TAIL: Yellow hackle fibres

RIB: Flat medium silver tinsel

BODY: Black floss

THROAT: Yellow cock hackle fibres

WING: White bucktail or bleached squirrel

CHEEKS: Optional – Jungle cock or substitute

The Black Ghost is just one member of a whole family of lures that were originally developed in the U.S.A. for Rainbow trout and Steelhead (sea-run Rainbow trout). Most of these patterns were originally tied with whole feather hackle wings, but in the modern versions this has been supplanted by hair which is more mobile and does not have the tendency to twist around the fly in the same way as a feather wing.

In the United Kingdom this type of lure became very popular at the beginning of the explosion in stillwater fishing for stocked rainbow trout. Since that time a vast number of deriva-tives have been produced, but some of the original patterns, like the Black Ghost, retain their popularity and also their effectiveness.

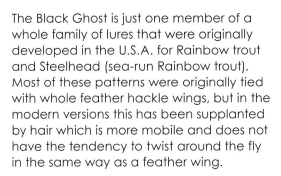

The choice of winging material is to a large extent dependent upon the size of the fly. Squirrel hair is often used for the smaller sizes, but for larger flies Bucktail may be a better choice. Bucktail fibres have a natural crinkle and if this is not too exaggerated this is a positive feature. The hair for the wing may be stacked, to even up the lengths (see **Hair Stacking**, page 64), but some tyers prefer to use only their fingers so as to leave the hair less tidy, producing a more tapered-looking wing. The choice is yours, but remember, which-ever method you choose, the fluffy under-hair must be removed.

Among other variants of this type of lure, the Mrs. Palmer, illustrated below, which was devised by the late Richard Walker, one of the pioneers of stillwater trout fishing in the United Kingdom, is still a superbly effective pattern for coloured water.

Jungle cock cheeks are given as optional extras but there is no doubt that they add considerably to the effectiveness of the flies. The problem with jungle cock is the price – it is very expensive indeed.

Artificial substitutes have long been used, mostly small black feathers with hand-painted dots, but these are not totally convincing.

Probably the best substitutes available to date are those which are accurate photo-graphic reproductions of real feathers, printed onto plastic.

BLACK GHOST – a hairwing lure

Step-by-Step Tying Instructions

STEP 1

Set the hook in the vice, taking hold only of the bend of the hook. Run the thread from a position about 3mm (1/8") behind the eye of the hook back to a point above the barb, in close touching turns.

STEP 2

Now catch in a bunch of the hackle fibres for the tail. They should extend about the same length as the hook gape from the tying-in point and should lie on the top of the hook shank. Don't cut off the waste ends at this stage as this will make a step in the body. The waste ends will be tied down when we wind the thread forward.

STEP 3

The silver ribbing and floss are now tied in at the same point above the barb. When you tie in these materials, take account of the hook length and make sure that you have enough. Wind the tying thread forward to the first tying-in position.

STEP 4

Form the floss body, trying to make it as smooth as possible. If you want a slightly heavier body you could bring the tying thread forward after you have tied in the ribbing and tie in the floss at the head end of the fly. You can then wind the body floss back to the tail position and then forward again before securing and cutting away the waste

STEP 5

Now for the rib. This is wound forwards in even, open turns finishing at the first position about 2 to 3 mm (1/8") away from the hook eye. Depending upon the hook length, five to seven turns are about right. Secure with 2 or 3 turns of thread and cut away the waste.

STEP 6

The beard hackle can now be applied. Take a bunch of the hackle fibres and apply them to the underside of the hook at the tying-in position, taking 1 or 2 turns of thread to hold them in position. If necessary at this stage you can use your fingers to distribute the fibres around the hook shank. Check the distribution of the fibres from the rear of the hook as well. For a full explanation of this procedure see **Beard Hackles** on page 22. You can turn the hook upside down in the vice to do this if you prefer, but if you can learn to work without doing so, it will save an unnecessary move.

STEP 7

Prepare the winging material by cleaning out the underfur. Either use a hair stacker so that the tips of the wing have an even length or use your fingers for a more tapered look. Offer up the wing fibres on top of the hookshank so that the wing is as long as the hook. Take a couple off turns to hold the wing in position and check the length. If it is satisfactory, make a few more tight turns to secure the wing. Now lift the wing and take one turn around the base of the wing fibres so that they stay together as a bunch, rather than spreading around the hook shank, Take two more turns in front and then trim away the waste fibres at an angle just in front of the eye. All these procedures are explained in detail in the section **Hair Wings** on page 26.

STEP 8

If you wish to use the optional Jungle Cock cheeks, they can be tied in now on either side of the wing. A neat head can then be formed by wrapping the thread over the wing butts to form a bullet shape. Finally give the head a shiny finish with two coats of varnish.

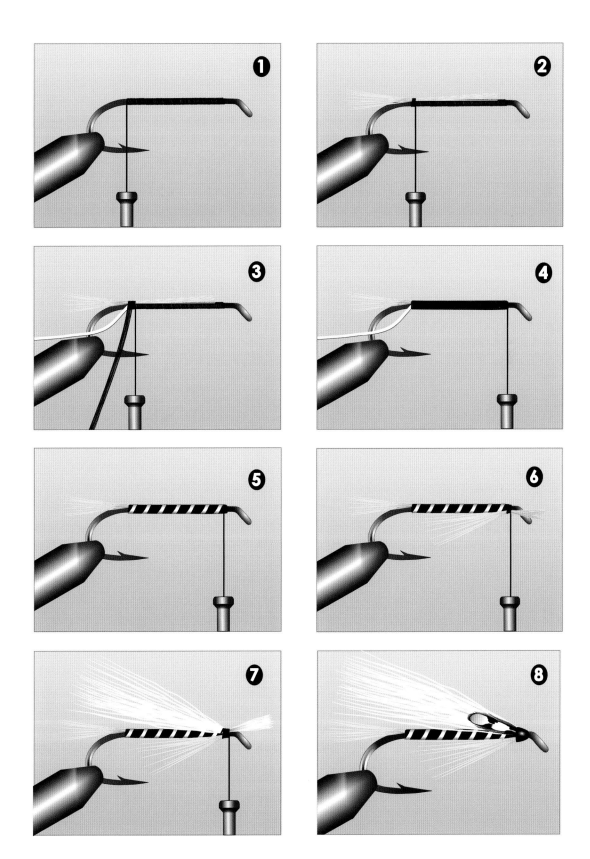

TRICKS OF THE TRADE 3: A SENSE OF PROPORTION

For almost every style of fly, wet, dry or nymph, there is an ideal proportion that is generally accepted as being correct because they catch fish, and also because they look good. The fact that a fly looks attractive to our eyes should not be dismissed as being irrelevant. It is a fact that anglers fish better with flies that they like. The generally accepted proportions can be varied according to personal preference – but within limits. The diagrams below are not intended to be hard rules. They do however show you the range of normal variations which you can use as a guide for your own tying.

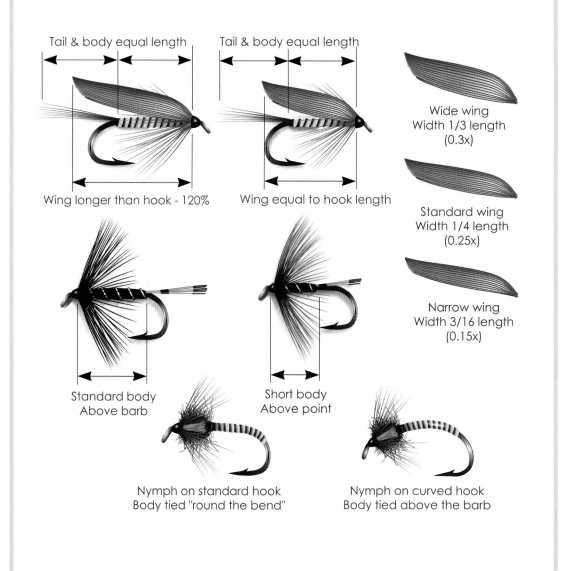

Tail & body equal length

Wing longer than hook - 120%

Tail & body equal length

Wing equal to hook length

Wide wing
Width 1/3 length
(0.3x)

Standard wing
Width 1/4 length
(0.25x)

Narrow wing
Width 3/16 length
(0.15x)

Standard body
Above barb

Short body
Above point

Nymph on standard hook
Body tied "round the bend"

Nymph on curved hook
Body tied above the barb

PHEASANT TAIL – a simple classic nymph

MATERIALS

HOOK: Long shank lure hook size 6-10

THREAD: Black 6/0, 8/0 for smaller sizes

TAIL: Pheasant tail fibres

RIB: Fine copper wire

WING CASE: Cock pheasant tail fibres

BODY: Cock pheasant tail fibres

THORAX: Cock pheasant tail fibres

The Pheasant Tail Nymph is one of the all-time classic nymphs for both stillwaters and rivers. Not a specific imitation of any particular species, it serves as a general suggestive imitator of a whole range of food items and is effective in all conditions and at all times of the year. For the beginner to flyfishing it is often difficult to have confidence in such a small, nondescript fly. One wonders if the trout can even see it, let alone be moved to take it. On this score you need have no fear: trout can certainly see it and will take it with confidence. The very fact that it is not flashy means that it does not cause any suspicion in the fish.

With such a widespread and successful pattern it should not surprise you to learn that there are literally thousands of variations on the Pheasant Tail theme. Perhaps the best known is Frank Sawyer's Pheasant Tail nymph. In this version the thorax consists solely of wound copper wire with a wing case over.

The main material for this fly (and for many other similar flies) is fibres from the centre tail feathers of a cock pheasant. In Europe this will normally be the common or Ring-Necked Pheasant; in the USA it may be from other similar species.

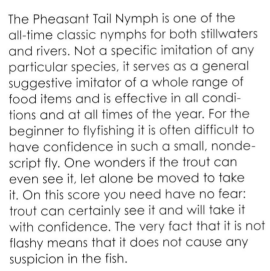

Pheasant tails come in a whole range of natural colours and markings, and dyed materials extend the range even further. The wide variation in the natural colours is clear from the accompanying picture. The colour of the nymph can obviously be varied by the selection of the fibres from which it is tied.

The thorax of the Pheasant Tail Nymph can be varied – in our example we have used pheasant tail fibres but you can also make the thorax simply of the copper wire or even apply a light dubbing of seal's fur in various colours.

One important point – you will often see commercial tyings with a bulbous thorax. This is not correct – nymphs are slender creatures and your fly should reflect this.

PHEASANT TAIL – a simple classic nymph

Step-by-Step Tying Instructions

STEP 1
Set the hook in the vice, taking hold only of the bend of the hook. From a position about 2-3mm (1/8") from the eye, run the thread back to a point above the barb, in close touching turns.

STEP 2
At this point you should tie in a good length of copper wire. Make sure you have enough – say about 250 to 300mm (9 - 12") long, and tie it in securely.

STEP 3
Select a bunch of pheasant tail fibres for the tail. The length of these fibres will vary according to the pheasant tail that you have. For the smaller sizes of fly they may be long enough to form the body as well as the tail. In this exercise we shall presume that this is not so, and that the tail will be separate from the body. Tie in the tails so that they extend backwards from the tying-in point by about half the hook length. Secure with a few turns of thread and cut away the waste ends.

STEP 4
Now select another bunch of fibres for the body and tie them in by their tips with two or three turns of thread. Wind the tying thread forward to a position about 2/3rds of the way along the hook shank.

STEP 5
Wind the bunch of body fibres forwards in even, non-overlapping turns to the 2/3rds position, to form a slim tapered body. Bring the fibres round to the top of the fly and tie them off with two turns of thread but do not cut away the ends – we will need them again later on.

STEP 6
Now take the copper wire forwards in even, open turns to the same position. At this stage you can take additional turns of the copper wire over the thorax area to add some weight to the fly if desired. The thorax can be left simply as turns of wire or you can add some seal's fur dubbing. In our case we shall tie in an additional bunch of pheasant tail fibres.

STEP 7
After tying in the new pheasant tail fibres, wind the tying thread forwards to the eye position and follow this with the pheasant tail fibres that you have just tied in. Secure the ends with two or three turns of thread and cut away the excess. It is important that you do not overdo the material for the thorax – at all costs you should avoid a bulbous look. You will see many commercial tyings that look as if they have a football behind the head – this is totally incorrect. No real nymph has such a shape.

STEP 8
Now take hold of the bunch of fibres that were left over from the body – remember, we didn't cut them off earlier. Stretch the fibres forwards over the thorax to form the wing case. At the eye position, secure them with several tight turns of thread and cut away the excess. Form a small head with some more turns of thread and a whip finish. A drop or two of varnish will complete the fly.

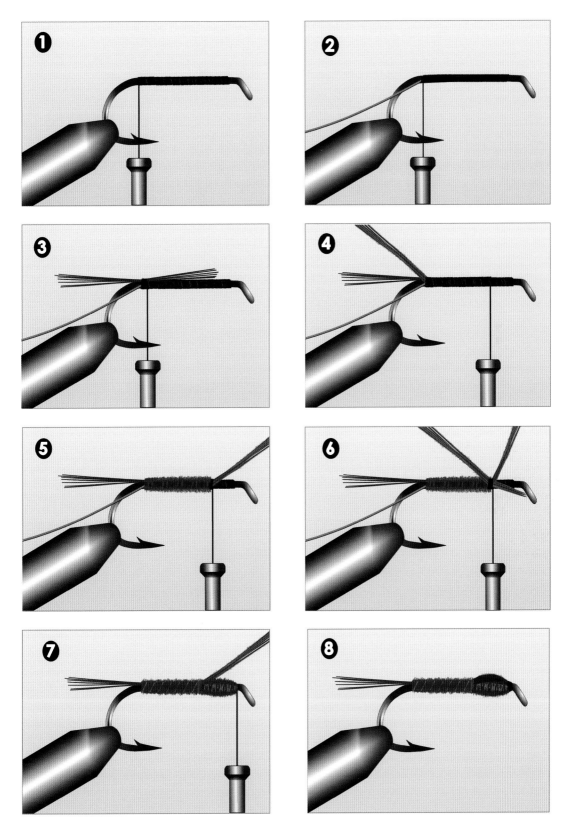

With any fly, the look can be altered considerably by varying the lengths and bulk of the materials. The features that have the most visual impact are the length and width of the wing, the length of the tail and the length of the hackle. The pictures below show a wide range of styles for the same fly. As you can see, stylistic differences are acceptable providing that they stay within limits. Changing the hook type can also have a major impact upon the appearance of the fly. In the figures below you can see that the flies tied on the long shank hooks have a more elegant appearance than the more business-like tyings on the standard hooks. The two flies at the bottom show how things can sometimes go wrong.

Standard dressing on a long
shank hook. Elegant & streamlined

Dressed shorter on the same hook.
Not so elegant, but still good

Dressed on a standard hook.
Business-like and in proportion

Dressed with the wing slips mounted
curve down. Unusual, but why not?

This has gone totally wrong - wing
and tail are far too long

This one has gone the other way.
It would suit a hook 2 sizes smaller

ELK HAIR CADDIS – a surface-effect dry fly

MATERIALS

HOOK: Down eyed lightweight dry-fly hook size 10-16

THREAD: Rusty brown 6/0

RIB: Fine gold wire

BODY: Hare's fur, taken from the mask

HACKLE: Natural red cock hackle

WING: Natural or bleached Elk body hair

To understand the reason for the shape of this fly you have to understand a little of the natural history of the Caddis Fly. When a Caddis Fly pupa hatches, the emergent adult swims as fast as it can to reach the bank – and safety. Whilst engaged in this mad dash for survival, it creates a vee-shaped wake rather like a miniature speedboat. The trout, who find Caddis very much to their taste, are well aware of this give-away feature and home in on the fly with some of the most spectacular takes which can be experienced.

The Elk-Hair Caddis imitates this fly in two ways – firstly the hair wing imitates the roof shaped, flat lying wing of the Caddis fly very well; secondly the blunt stubs of the wing cause a commotion and wake on the surface when the fly is retrieved which exactly mimics the behaviour of the natural.

Caddis flies are at home on both still and running waters and at all stages of their lives provide an important source of food for the trout, especially in the larval form.

A common variation of the Elk Hair Caddis has a fluorescent green or yellow butt which imitates the egg cluster of the female fly as she returns to the water to lay her eggs.

In this case the fly is fished in a more static way. This version of the fly is extremely effective in the late evening.

The Elk hair used for the wing of this fly is fairly incompressible and thus will not flare when it is tied in.

ELK HAIR CADDIS – a surface-effect dry fly

Step-by-Step Tying Instructions

STEP 1

Set the hook in the vice and from a position about 3mm (1/8") behind the eye, run the thread back to a point above the barb, in close touching turns. At this point, tie in a length of fine gold wire for the ribbing (about 10cm - 4" long is ideal).

STEP 2

Load a small quantity of dubbing by teasing out a small quantity of the hare's fur. Offer this material up to the thread and by twisting with the thumb and forefinger, in one direction only, form a spindle of material. Don't use too much material. As a rule, when you think you have enough dubbing, halve it! Instructions on this procedure are given under **Dubbing** on page 19.

STEP 3

Wind the dubbing forwards to the starting position and secure with a couple of turns. Remove any excess material from the thread. At this point you should tie in the cock hackle by its stalk, having prepared it in the usual manner.

STEP 4

Take the tip of the hackle in the hackle pliers and take two turns at the tying-in position. Follow this with a series of even, open turns backwards to the rear position. At this position, leave the hackle hanging with the hackle pliers still attached, and take two turns of the rib over the hackle to trap it down. When it is secure, remove the hackle pliers and trim away the waste.

STEP 5

Now take the end of the ribbing between your finger and thumb and wind it forward, through the hackle in the opposite spiral, trapping down the hackle stalk at each turn.

Try not to tie down the hackle fibres themselves – you will find that the easiest way to avoid this is to wiggle the ribbing backwards and forwards as you wind it. When you reach the front, secure the ribbing with two turns of thread and trim away the excess.

STEP 6

The wing fibres should be prepared by combing out the fluff at the base and then using a hair stacker to ensure that the tips are even. Using the thumb and forefinger, offer up the bunch of fibres to the hook, setting the tips of the wing at about level with the hook bend. With the wing in this position take three or four turns of thread around the wing. Note that these first turns are not intended to secure the wing, but rather to position it. The turns should be firm enough to hold the wing in position but do not have to be very tight.

STEP 7

Release the wing and check it for length. If everything is in position take hold of the wing again and make three or four more tight turns of thread in front of the previous turns. Try to keep these turns on top of one another so that they form a neat binding. Keep a firm hold on the wing as you secure it, otherwise you will find that it will tend to rotate around the hook shank. Cut the butts ends of the wing away with a vertical cut directly above the hook eye.

STEP 8

Finally, with your scissors, trim away the butt ends at an angle, following the slope of the eye. Now apply several coats of thinned varnish to the wing butts and the collar of thread – this will secure everything and the stiffened butts will help to cause the wake when fishing the fly.

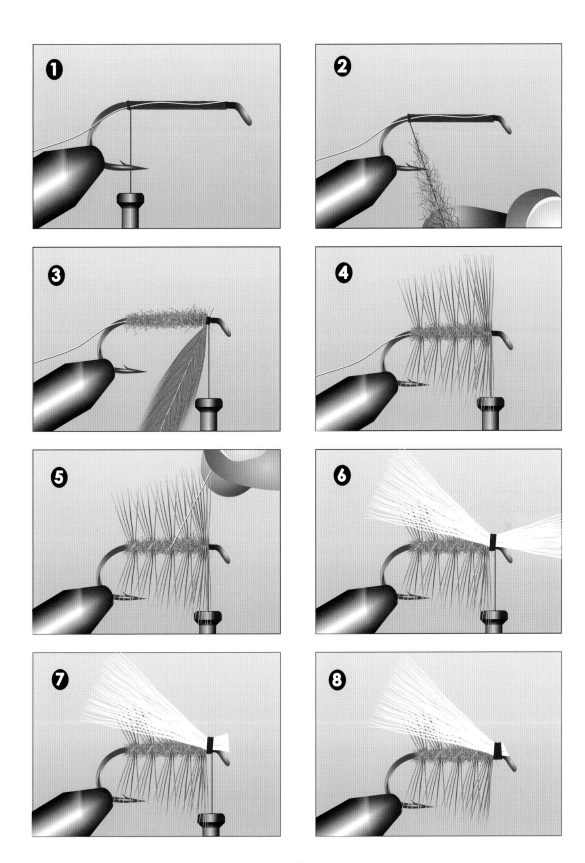

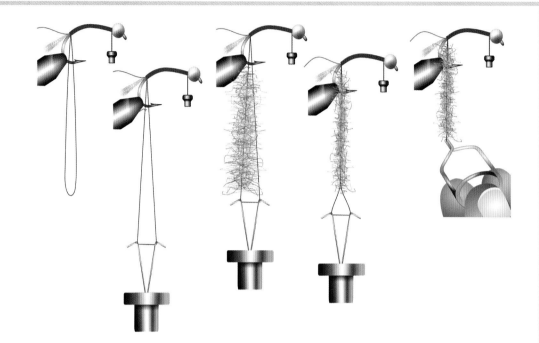

The dubbing loop is ideal when you wish to produce long, straggly dubbing or are using a material that does not easily adhere to the thread. The more off-centre the dubbing fibres are set in the loop, the longer will be the fibres in the finished body. This technique can also be used to make hair fibre 'hackles' – super for small nymphs with a lot of life and 'kick' in the water.

STEP 1
Make a loop in the tying thread and, having secured it, wind the tying thread out of the way

STEP 2
Introduce the twirler into the loop

STEP 3
With a stick of flytyer's wax, lightly wax the inside of the loop. Not too much; you don't want lumps of wax

STEP 4
Tease out a pinch of dubbing and spread the material evenly along the inside of the loop

STEP 5
Give the dubbing twirler a good spin with your thumb and forefinger

STEP 6
Clip your hackle pliers on to the bottom of the loop. When this is done, the loop can no longer untwist and you can remove the twirler

STEP 7
Wind the dubbing on to the hook in even turns without overlapping them

STEP 8
When you reach the head, tie off the dubbing loop with a couple of turns of tying thread and then cut away the excess

GINGER QUILL – a classic wet fly

MATERIALS

HOOK: Standard wet fly hook size 8-12

THREAD: Brown 6/0

TAIL: Ginger/light natural red

BODY: Hackle fibres

HACKLE: Stripped quill from peacock eye

WING: Ginger/natural light red cock hackle fibres

Slips taken from a matched pair of grey duck secondary wing quills

Good preparation work is the essence of consistent quality flytying. The materials should be prepared as follows.

The body of the Ginger Quill is formed by a quill from a Peacock eye feather (above) which has been stripped of its flue. The quill has a light and a dark stripe along it which gives the beautifully segmented body appearance.

The quill can be stripped of its flue in two ways. The first method is to wet the flue thoroughly with saliva and leave it for a few minutes. Trap the quill between your thumb nail and first finger and draw them along the length. This removes the flue and polishes the quill at the same time. An alternative is to coat the quill with Copydex and after a few minutes, rub it off. The flue will be removed along with the Copydex.

The wings are made of two slips of Grey Duck wing (below), taken from the same position from two opposing wing quills. Ensure that the two slips are of equal width.

GINGER QUILL – a classic wet fly

Step-by-Step Tying Instructions

STEP 1

Set the hook in the vice, taking hold only of the bend of the hook. Run the thread from just behind the eye of the hook to a point above the barb, in close touching turns.

STEP 2

Now catch in a small bunch of the hackle fibres for the tail. They should be about the same length as the body and should lie on the top of the hook shank. Don't cut off the waste ends at this stage as this will make a step in the body. The waste ends will be tied down when we wind the thread forward.

STEP 3

Tie in the stripped Peacock quill at a point directly above the barb. Try to tie the quill in so that when you wrap it, the darker side of the quill will be at the back, nearer the hook bend. Now continue to wind the thread back towards the hook eye making an even base layer on which the quill will be wound. Stop about 2-3mm (1/8") short of the hook eye.

STEP 4

The Peacock quill can now be wrapped forward in close touching turns. Again stop about 2mm (1/8") short of the eye, tie off with two or three turns of the thread and cut off the waste quill.

STEP 5

Tie in the hackle by the stalk, presenting the 'best' side to the shank, using two or three turns of thread.

STEP 6

Make two or three turns of the hackle and tie off using three turns of thread at most. The hackle should be swept back as shown, but not drawn under the shank.

STEP 7

The wing slips should be held in position between the thumb and forefinger and offered up to the hook shank for length, dull side to dull side / concave to concave. The wing should extend at least to the bend of the hook, but slightly longer will give a more elegant look. Once the length is established, take a turn of thread up over the wing between your fingers, passing down the other side, without any tension on the wing segment. This is called the pinch and loop method. The 'pinch' between the thumb and forefingers should be loose enough so as to allow the thread to pass between. For a full explanation of this procedure see **Pinch & Loop** on Page 25.

STEP 8

Now bring the thread up at the front, again between the two fingers. Tension can now be applied to the thread in an upward direction as shown in figure 8. The whole idea of this procedure is to apply tension to the wing segments in a vertical direction, so that the feather fibres have no tendency to roll and split, but compress tidily one on top of another.

STEP 9

A quick look will tell you if the wing is set correctly. If it is, make a few turns, but no more than half a dozen, to secure it.

STEP 10

Trim off the waste ends of the wing butts as closely as possible and finish the head with neat turns of thread. Make secure by either whipping or take a couple of half-hitches. Complete the head with a careful coat of varnish.

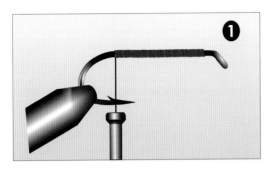

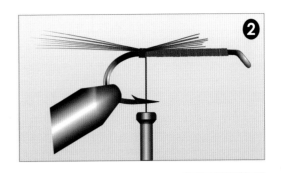

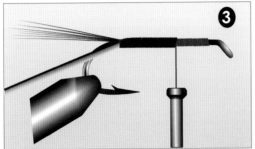

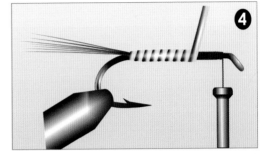

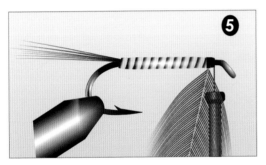

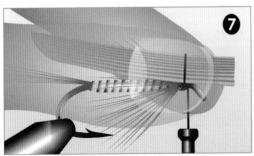

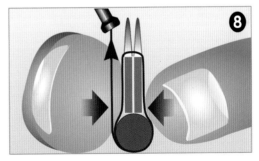

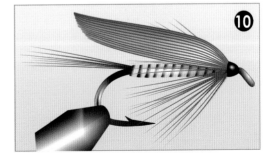

TRICKS OF THE TRADE 6: TOUGH TINSEL

Tinsel bodies, even when they are correctly tied, can be a source of weakness in a fly. This is particularly the case when the tinsel being used is of the Lurex type. This modern type of tinsel has many advantages over the traditional metal but strength is not one of its best features. You can make all tinsel bodies much more robust by the judicious use of varnish during the tying procedure. A bit of patience is called for here because you must let the varnish go tacky before winding over it – if you don't do this, it is easy to end up with a sticky mess. Note also that a thin layer of varnish is called for – if it forms drops on the hook shank, you have used too much. One last tip – don't be tempted to use your fingers. If you do, you will quickly transfer the varnish onto your tools and other materials. You can use this technique to strengthen herl bodies as well.

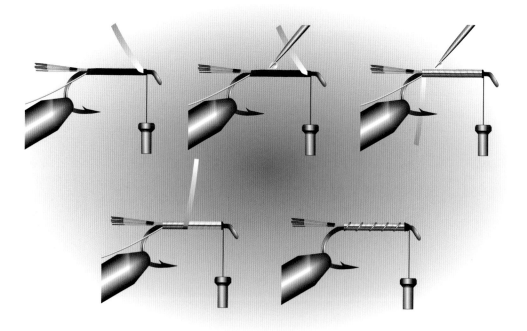

Apply a layer of varnish over the thread before winding the tinsel to the rear. Apply the next coat of varnish over this tinsel. When it is tacky, wind the second layer of tinsel forwards and tie off at the head. Ribbing will also help to secure the tinsel body.

A final coating of varnish can also be given for the ultimate in tough tinsel bodies. This will also stop the tinsel tarnishing if it is of the traditional metal type.

GOLDHEAD HARE'S EAR – a fast sinking nymph

MATERIALS

HOOK: Curved grub hook size 8-14

THREAD: Rusty brown 6/0

BEAD: 2 or 3mm (1/8") brass bead

TAIL: A bunch of hare's mask guard hairs

RIB: Fine gold wire

BODY: Hare's fur taken from the mask (face)

The Gold-Ribbed Hare's Ear (or GRHE as it is often called) is one of the classic all purpose nymph patterns and has been around for many years. To our eyes the hare's fur may seem pretty nondescript but it seems to have a fatal fascination for trout of all species.

Because of its widespread success, the GRHE has spawned a whole family of variants. Almost all of these flies share the same body – hare's fur ribbed with gold wire – although the other details may vary. Some have a separated thorax, with or without a wing case, others may sport some kind of winging.

One of the great success stories in modern flyfishing is the application of bead heads to standard patterns. The beads may be gold, silver, copper or even plastic or glass of various colours.

The features that make these patterns so effective can be summarised as follows: the bead provides weight which sinks the fly to a fishable depth very quickly (and keeps it there). The weight at the front provides an undulating movement in the water flow or when the fly is retrieved. The flash of the bead mimics the gas bubble which is a feature of ascending pupae of many fly species.

The GRHE is an outstanding candidate for this treatment – a gold bead beautifully matching the body colour and the gold sparkle of the ribbing. In practice the Goldhead GRHE fulfills all the expectations, and is one of the most effective nymph patterns of modern times. It can be used in all conditions and at all times of the season. There are few patterns that are truly indispensable: the GRHE and its gold-headed variant are such patterns.

It should be noted that although the classic dressing calls for hare's fur taken from the ear, the fur may be taken from any part of the hare's mask (face). The important thing is to get a range of colours and include a lot of the longer guard hairs. If your fly looks neat when it is tied, it's wrong!

GOLDHEAD HARE'S EAR – a fast sinking nymph

Step-by-Step Tying Instructions

STEP 1

For this fly, some work is needed before we set place the hook in the vice. Take the gold bead and slide it on to the hook from the hook point end, with the countersunk side towards the eye. Putting the bead on this way round will slightly mask the hook eye as it will recess into the countersink. There will still be plenty of room to the thread the hook and the countersink at the front gives added movement in the water.

Once the bead is on the hook you can set the hook in the vice, taking hold only of the bend of the hook. The bead is now glued into position. Slide the bead back out of the way and apply a drop of superglue to the hook shank behind the eye and then slide the bead forwards again into position.

From a position directly behind the bead, run the thread back to a point above the barb, in close touching turns.

STEP 2

Now tie in the tail fibres. Select a bunch of guard hairs from the hare's fur. The guard hairs are the longer stiffer, fibres. Tie them in to lie round the bend of the hook as shown. When this is done you should tie in a length of fine gold wire or oval tinsel to act as a rib.

STEP 3

Now form a loop in the thread about 10cm (4") long and then take the thread back up to the rear of the bead. A dubbing twister should then be set in the loop to hold it open. Lightly wax the thread on the inside of the loop (there should be no lumpy residue on the thread). Tease out the hare's fur and apply it along the inside of the loop – there should be plenty of the longer guard hairs in this mix. Try and spread the dubbing mixture out evenly.

STEP 4

Now comes the clever bit. Take hold of the dubbing twirler between thumb and forefinger and give it a spin. This spinning will trap the applied dubbing between the two strands of thread and produce a hairy 'rope'. A dubbing rope of this sort is ideal when you wish to produce a body with lots of 'kick'. The dubbed body of the hare's ear should be slim but straggly with plenty of longer hairs to give movement in the water. It is difficult to produce this effect, applying the fibres to a single strand of thread.

STEP 5

The next step is to wind the dubbing rope forwards in even turns. Before doing this, I find it easier to grip the end of the dubbing rope in the hackle pliers. Once this is done, the rope can no longer untwist and the twirler may be removed.

STEP 6

Take the dubbing forwards, ending up tight behind the gold bead (this will also help to hold the bead in place if the glue fails after some use). Pull the last turn tight in and then secure the end of the rope with two turns of the tying thread. Remember, we left it there when we first formed the dubbing rope. When the rope is tied down you can trim away any excess with a sharp pair of scissors.

STEP 7

Now wind the rib forward in even, open turns, pulling it quite tightly into the dubbed body. When you reach the rear of the gold bead, again secure it with a couple of turns of thread and cut away the waste. The tying thread should then be made secure with several whip finish turns or half-hitches. A drop of varnish will finish off the fly.

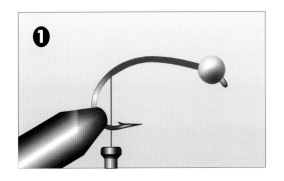

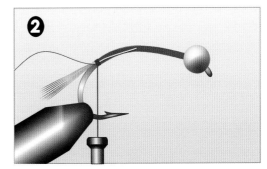

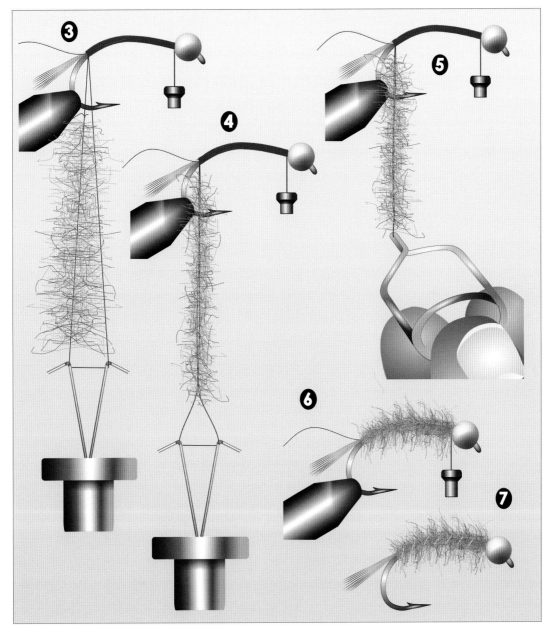

TRICKS OF THE TRADE 7: VARNISHING THE HEAD

Achieving neatly-varnished heads is often the bane of new tyers. So, for the beginner, here are a few tips which may help. Firstly, let's consider the varnish.

Don't try to apply a varnish that has thickened up! If the varnish has thickened (which it does) take a drop of the appropriate thinner, and thin it progressively, taking the mixture down to a liquid consistency only a little thicker than water. Apply this varnish and it will soak through the thread and will act more as a glue than as a glossy surface.

Forget all about brushes! Apply the varnish with as fine a needle as you can find. You will usually find that it takes anything from three to four individual drops on the tip of the needle to complete one coating on a size 10 hook. This thin varnish acts as a primer. Thicker varnish can be applied subsequently over this.

When applying cement or lacquer to larger flies, build up the coatings slowly. Wait for each coat to dry before applying subsequent ones. If you don't wait, you'll achieve the 'prune' effect where a heavy build-up will wrinkle – almost impossible to fix.

For most varnishing jobs you should use a good quality cellulose such as Veniards' Cellire – it can also be thinned for use as a primer. An acrylic such as Firefly Liquid Glass or Hard-As-Nails clear nail varnish is ideal for a protective, hard finish. The latter two are quite viscous, will hold a good 'body' and give a high gloss finish. With these high quality acrylics readily available we don't see much point in messing about with twin-pack epoxies, especially since the drying time can be extremely long.

Don't apply black (or any other colour) head cement directly over new head whippings. Even with the greatest of care, the black has the unhappy knack of leeching onto feather or hair fibre, transforming a neat finish into an untidy mess. Use the thinned clear varnish as the primer and follow this with the black in small, successive applications. Use black varnish only when absolutely necessary. Clear varnish over black thread is better.

If, after making your 'perfect' fly some light coloured fibres in the head have not been totally covered by the thread – don't despair! Use a fine black waterproof marker pen to blacken the rogue fibres, then apply clear varnish. This avoids the build-up of unnecessary turns of thread.

GREY WULFF – a classic hairwing dry fly

MATERIALS

HOOK: Down-eyed medium weight dry-fly hook size 6-14

THREAD: Rusty brown 6/0

WING: Natural brown bucktail

TAIL: Natural brown bucktail

BODY: Grey muskrat or rabbit underfur

HACKLE: Two blue dun cock hackles

This American fly from Lee Wulff is a classic fast-water dry fly that is indispensable to fishermen throughout the world. On the chalk streams of the United Kingdom the Grey Wulff is synonymous with the Mayfly but in fact it is representative of a great variety of duns and other insects. One of the classic patterns and arguably one of the top ten dry flies ever conceived.

Not surprisingly the original pattern Grey Wulff has spawned a whole range of variants, the best known of which are the Royal Wulff, the Grizzle Wulff and the Black Wulff. As a consequence of the success of the Wulff-style of dressing, the use of hair as a winging material for dry flies has spread widely and in many cases has replaced the traditional upright split wings made of feather slips. The difficulty of tying traditional wings of this type has much to do with the increased popularity of hair wings. The fish however do not seem to mind greatly which method is used.

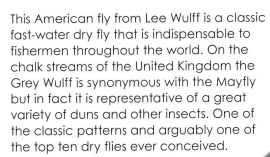

In our tying, the wing consists of a single bunch of hair. Purists will point out that a dry fly has two wings. The process of binding the roots of the wing together, as described in step 3 of the dressing instruc-

tions can indeed be extended to divide the wing into two separate bunches, thus forming a classic split wing but It is doubtful if this feature actually improves the fishing quality of the fly.

The hackle used for the Grey Wulff is a medium Blue Dun cock. For flies in the sizes 6 - 14 the best value that can be obtained is to invest in a genetic saddle from one of the top names such as Metz or Hoffman. A grade 2 or 3 saddle costs only a fraction of the price of a neck cape and will contain feathers up to 200mm (8") long. Just one of these feathers will tie many flies.

GREY WULFF – a classic hairwing dry fly

Step-by-Step Tying Instructions

STEP 1

Set the hook in the vice and from a position about 3mm (1/8") behind the eye, run the thread back to a point above the barb, in close touching turns.

STEP 2

Select a bunch of bucktail for the wing and prepare it by cleaning out any underfur from the butt ends. Once this has been done the hair should be placed in a hair stacker and the tips evened up as explained on page 64. Offer the bucktail up to the hook with **the tips pointing forwards** over the eye (the opposite way to a normal wing) by about the hook-shank length from the tying-in position. Take four or five turns of thread to hold the hair in position and then check for length.

STEP 3

If the hair is the correct length, take some more turns to fasten it securely. Set the wing by lifting up the hair and taking several turns of thread tight in front. This should cause the wing to sit almost upright, but with a forward lean. Take a few turns of thread around the base of the wing itself so that it holds together then cut off the ends of the hair at an angle as shown. A few drops of varnish on the base of the wing will make it more secure. Return the thread to the rear of the hook with just a few turns to hold the cut ends of the wing.

STEP 4

We can now tie in the tail. Prepare the hair in the same way as for the wing. Tie in the tail and check for length. When you are satisfied, take a couple of turns more to secure the tail. Now cut off the ends of the tail hair at an angle opposite to that used on the wing, so that the two dovetail neatly together as shown in the diagram.

STEP 5

Bring the tying thread forward in touching turns to the base of the wing and back again to the tail, forming a neat tapered base for the dubbing.

STEP 6

Load the dubbing by teasing out a small quantity of muskrat or rabbit underfur. Offer this material up to the thread and by twisting with the thumb and forefinger, in one direction only, form a spindle of material. Wind the dubbing forwards to the wing roots and secure with a couple of turns. Remove any excess material from the thread. The trick with dubbing is not to use too much material. Instructions on this procedure are given on page 19 **Dubbing**.

STEP 7

Take two blue dun cock hackles with a hackle length of about 1½ times the hook gape, which are matched for size and having trimmed away the flue at the bases, set them back to back. Tie these hackles in together at a position just behind the wing root. Keeping the two hackles even, grip the tips together in the hackle pliers and make two complete turns behind the wing and one turn in front of the wing

STEP 8

Tie down the ends of the hackles with a couple of turns of thread and trim away the waste. A few turns of thread will make a neat head. Secure the thread with a whip finish or half hitches and finish off with a few drops of varnish, Be careful here! You do not want the varnish to run into the hackle. Either use your fingers or a hackle guard, to hold the hackle back out of the way whilst you apply the varnish.

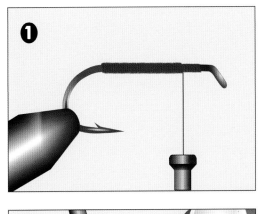

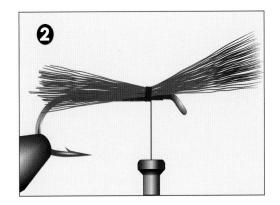

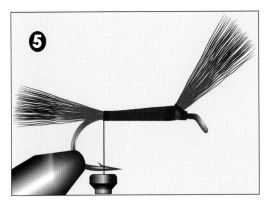

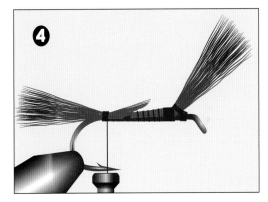

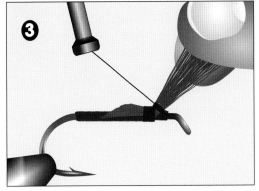

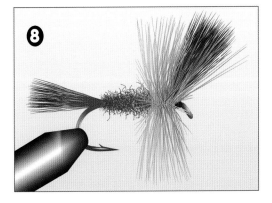

TRICKS OF THE TRADE 8: HACKLING HINTS

In the **Basic Flytying Techniques** section of the book (page 20) we looked at a range of hackling techniques. The following tips may help you with various aspects of these techniques.

Tying in the hackle stalk

You may find that there is a tendency for the hackle stalk to pull out from its windings, particularly when you start to wind the hackle. Two things can help here. Firstly, use your finger and thumbnail (or the back of your scissors) to flatten the hackle stalk below the hackle fibres. Ensure that you flatten it in the plane of the fibres. The tying thread will grip better and the stalk will take up less room. Secondly, you can use your finger and thumbnail to make a kink in the hackle stalk at the tying-in position. This will make a groove which will locate the tying thread and make things more secure.

Doubling a hackle

You may find that the hackle fibres simply don't want to fold back if you simply use your thumb and forefinger (see **Doubled Collar Hackle** on page 21). It can help if you prepare the hackle before it is tied in. Firstly, stroke the hackle fibres downwards, against the grain, until they sit at right angles to the spine. Now take the back edge of your scissors and run it along the top side of the hackle stalk towards the tip, gently but with sufficient pressure to 'break' the spine. The hackle fibres will now fold backwards more easily.

Stripping a hackle

A full hackle may sometimes be too bushy for the fly you are tying. This may be the case when you are using a palmered hackle (see **Palmered Hackles** on page 21) or when you are tying a 'spider' type pattern, where a wispy, sparse head hackle is called for.

In such cases you can strip the fibres from one side of the hackle stalk. To do this, grip the tip of the hackle in your left hand, making sure that you also have hold of the stalk. Now grip the fibres that need to be removed with the fingers of the right hand and strip them backwards, from the tip towards the butt end. If you do it correctly they will strip cleanly away from the spine, taking a small sliver of the spine material as well. The hackle can then be tied in and wound as usual.

This is also the correct way to select a bunch of hackle fibres for a tail or beard hackle – the sliver of spine helps keep the fibres together and they are much easier to handle.

TG PARACHUTE EMERGER – a hatching fly

MATERIALS

HOOK: Curved lightweight grub hook size 6-14

THREAD: Black 8/0

WING: Calf body hair or Polypropylene yarn

BODY: Cock pheasant tail fibres – natural, dyed black or claret

THORAX: Hot orange seal's fur, or substitute

HACKLE: Grizzle cock hackle

This is one of Terry's own patterns. It has been around for a few years but has not been widely publicised. The TG parachute emerger has proved equally effective for both brown and rainbow trout on the large stillwaters.

The picture above shows the TG Emerger sitting in the surface film. The 'angle of dangle' is critical to its success. This is set by the angle of the wing, so care must be taken to get this right.

The wing on this fly serves two important functions – firstly it acts as a post around which the parachute hackle is wound. Secondly it acts as an indicator when fishing. The colour of the wing is not actually critical but white shows up well against the water, enabling you to see where the fly is.

If you have difficulty managing the calf hair when tying the wing, you may find it easier to use polypropylene yarn instead. This is easier to control and in fishing terms, makes little difference.

Flies tied with parachute hackling float very well because the hackle fibres lie parallel to the surface film, rather than at right angles to it. Traditionally hackled flies stand on 'tippy toe' and the sharp cock hackles tend to penetrate the surface quite easily in anything but very calm water.

The great advantage of parachute hackles for emerger flies, is that the fly body hangs in the water at a natural angle, exactly imitating the natural fly as it struggles to emerge through the surface film.

TG PARACHUTE EMERGER – a hatching fly

Step-by-Step Tying Instructions

STEP 1
From a position just behind the eye, run the thread back, in close touching turns, along the front part of the hook to make a secure bed for the wing. Bring the thread back to the centre of the turns.

STEP 2
Now you can tie in the wing. Select a bunch of calf hair which is about 1.5mm (1/16") diameter. Clean out all the unwanted underhair and tie it in with three or four turns of thread, at about the 3mm (1/8") position so that it extends forwards about 1cm (3/8") over the eye.

STEP 3
The angle of the wing is critical for this fly because it dictates the angle at which the body will hang in the water. Lift the entire wing between thumb and forefinger and take a few turns of thread, tight in front of the wing to push it up at an angle of 45 degrees. With the wing held in position, take a few turns of thread around the base of the wing to bind it into a slim post.

STEP 4
Now cut away the butt ends of the wing fibres at an angle as shown. Now run the thread backwards in neat turns to the bend of the hook, binding in the loose ends as you go. You need to produce a neat tapered body. A drop of varnish on the wing root will help to secure everything.

STEP 5
A drop of varnish on the wing root will help to secure the wing and provide a good base for the hackle later

STEPS 6
At the end position, tie in a length of fine oval silver tinsel, followed by a bunch of pheasant tail fibres of the desired colour.

Bring the tying thread forward to the wing and then wind the pheasant tail forwards in neat turns. Tie off with two turns of thread. Follow this by winding the ribbing forwards in even, open turns. At the base of the wing, secure with a couple of turns of thread and cut away the waste of the ribbing and the pheasant tail.

STEP 7
Now tie in the grizzle hackle, pointing upwards next to the wing, as shown.

STEP 8
Take a small bunch of the thorax dubbing and wrap it sparsely around the thread. Take two turns behind the wing and one more in front, ending just in front of the wing. The thorax must not be bulky.

STEP 9
The parachute hackle can now be wound around the base of the wing. The first turn of the hackle will be the top one. All the rest will follow below this first turn. Take the tip of the hackle in the hackle pliers and make four turns in a clockwise direction, finishing with the tip pointing towards you. Now take the tying thread and twist it around the end of the hackle three or four times. Take the thread (with the entwined hackle tip) twice around the bottom of the wing stump. With the hackle secure you can remove the hackle pliers and cut away the excess hackle. Instructions for this procedure are given in the **Hackling** section on Page 20.

STEP 10
Take the tying thread forwards to the eye, beneath the hackle, and secure with half hitches (a whip finish would trap the hackle fibres). Carefully varnish the head.

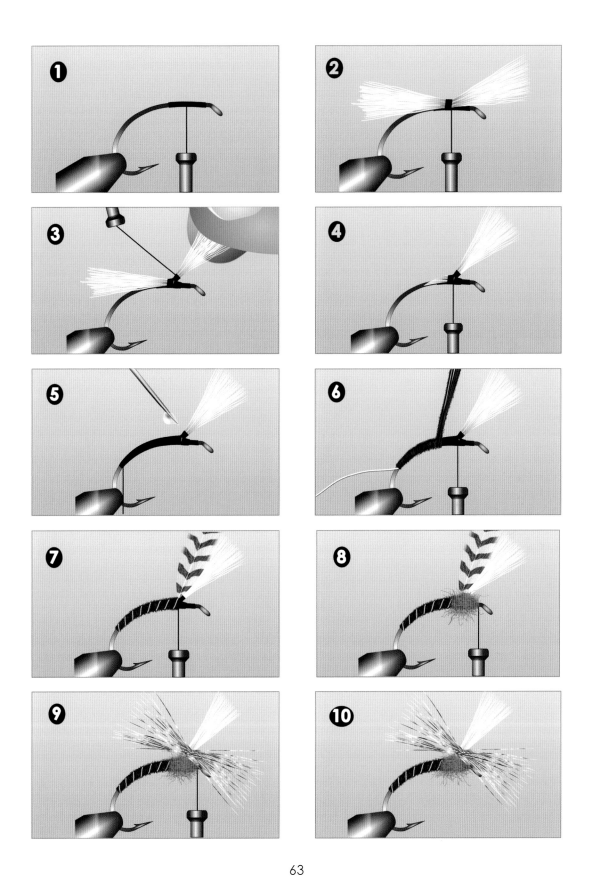

TRICKS OF THE TRADE 9: HAIR RAISING STUFF

When tails or wings consisting of hair are used in a fly pattern, the hair taken from the skin may sometimes be straggly and misaligned. In this case it is often necessary to even up the tips of the hair so that they form a coherent group. There are some tyers who find that perfectly even tips give a slightly artificial 'shaving brush' look to a fly. Actually, it depends on what kind of hair is being tied in, and for what purpose it is being used. The wing and tail of the Gray Wulff, illustrated on page 57, look much better if the hair tips are aligned. The same applies to the Elk Hair Caddis fly on page 43. Conversely, on hairwing lures such as the Black Ghost, there may be a case for a more unevenness, as the more tapered appearance of the fly may be more visually appealing.

There are many ways of evening up the tips of the hair, but the easiest and most consistent is by means of a hair stacker. Most hair stackers consist of two parts: an inner tube, and a base into which the tube fits. Using them is easy – the unordered hair is put tips down into the tube. The tube is put into the base and the whole assembly is tapped smartly on a hard surface. This sudden shock causes the tips of the hair to settle down evenly inside the base.

Do NOT do this on your unprotected dining room table!

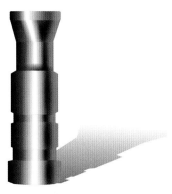

Commercially available hair stackers are usually made of brass or wood. It doesn't actually matter what the material is. What is important is that the inner surfaces are absolutely smooth. Some cheaper models are well finished outside, but rough within. The heavier the stacker, the greater the shock imparted to the hair, and the better it will settle down.

Cheaper alternatives can be made from old lipstick tubes or, for longer hair, plastic tubes of various kinds, previously occupied by tablets, sweets, cigars etc.

DUCK'S DUN – a modern thorax-style dry fly

MATERIALS

HOOK: Down-eye lightweight dry fly hook size 12-18

THREAD: Medium olive 8/0

TAIL: Blue dun or badger cock hackle fibres

BODY: Fine texture dubbing – bleached and dyed muskrat or synthetic

WING: Two natural Cul-de-Canard plumes

HACKLE: Blue dun cock hackle

The Duck's Dun is a modern dry fly dun imitation devised by Charles Jardine. There are two features of this fly that are of particular interest. Firstly, it is tied in the 'thorax' style – that is, the wing is tied in at the thorax position, some distance back from the hook eye. Secondly the wing consists of two CDC plumes. CDC (Cul-de-Canard) are fluffy filoplume feathers that come from around the preen gland of a duck. The preen gland supplies a copious flow of a natural oil which the duck uses to waterproof its feathers.

The plumes around the preen gland become saturated with this oil and are just about unsinkable.

In addition to their natural waterproofing, CDC plumes are well endowed with barbules which trap tiny bubbles of air, thus enhancing the floating qualities. Flies tied with CDC feathers are naturally buoyant and do not need treating with an artificial floatant. In the case of the Duck's Dun, however, we do not want the body to sink under the water at all, so the fly is normally treated with floatant.

The body colour of a Duck's Dun can be varied, depending upon the natural fly that is being imitated. Most commonly-used are shades of olive and brown.

The hackle on the Duck's Dun is normally clipped away beneath the hook shank quite short so that the fly sits flat in the surface film of the water just like the natural dun. The spiky effect created by the clipped hackle gives a 'fussy' dimpled footprint in the water.

The Duck's Dun is one of the very best of the modern generation of dry flies and has very quickly become one of the standard dressings for stream fishing, both in the USA and the United Kingdom.

DUCK'S DUN – a modern thorax-style dry fly

Step-by-Step Tying Instructions

STEP 1

Set the hook in the vice, taking hold only of the bend of the hook. From a position about 2-3mm (1/8") from the eye, run the thread back to a point above the barb, in close touching turns. Before you tie in the tail fibres, you need to put a tiny ball of the dubbing material (about 1mm - 1/16" diameter) on to the top of the hook at the tying-in position for the tail. This little ball of dubbing is used to split the tail fibres into two groups in a forked configuration.

STEP 2

Now for the tail fibres themselves – take the first bunch of two or three fibres and lay then onto the hook shank at the near side of the dubbing ball, using the ball as a shoulder so that the fibres splay outwards at an angle to the hook shank. When they are sitting correctly, take one or two turns of thread to secure them and then repeat the procedure for the fibres on the far side. Figure 2 shows the effect that you are trying to achieve.

STEP 3

Return the thread to the rear position and prepare a dubbing rope. Make sure that the dubbing is sparse and slim. Bring the dubbing forwards in even turns, making a slightly tapered body until you reach the tying-in position for the wing. At this stage remove the excess dubbing from the thread.

STEP 4

Now tie in the prepared cock hackle. This should be prepared and tied in as explained under **Hackling** on Page 20. The length of the hackle fibres should be a bit longer than the hook gape at the widest point.

STEP 5

The next step is to tie in the wing. Select two natural CDC plumes – these feathers need to be about 15-19 mm (1/2"-5/8") long measured from the tying-in position. Place the feathers tip to tip, convex side to convex side, so that there is a natural curve outwards. Place the feathers on edge, in position and take several turns around the butt ends to secure. Pull the first two of these turns in tight, so that the feathers are forced back against the shoulder of the dubbing. In this way the wing will cock up into position naturally at an angle of about 60 degrees. Trim away the butt ends and bring the thread back behind the wing.

STEP 6

At this point you should add some more dubbing to the thread and then wind one turn behind the wing, followed by two or three more turns in front, finishing just short of the eye.

STEP 7

Now take the tip of the hackle in the hackle pliers and after taking one turn behind the wing, wrap the hackle forwards through the thorax in even, open turns like a ribbing, keeping a steady tension as you do so. When you reach the front position, secure the hackle with two turns of thread and cut away the excess.

STEP 8

Finish the fly with several turns of thread, making a small neat head – do not overdo this. Make secure with a whip finish and complete the head with a drop or two of varnish. Lastly, with your scissors, trim away the hackle lying underneath the hook shank.

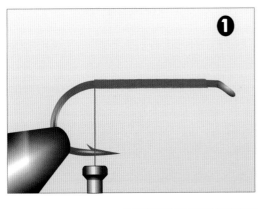

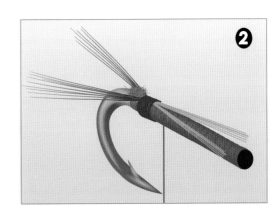

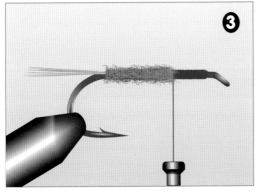

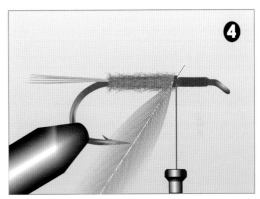

Materials need to be stored in an orderly way if you wish to find the things you need, when you need them. There are very expensive, custom-made wooden storage cabinets available. These are beautiful but fortunately, not absolutely necessary. As a low-cost alternative, a series of cardboard archive boxes (used for storing documents and available from most office supplies shops) can be quite satisfactory. The individual feathers, furs and other materials can be kept in re-sealable plastic bags and simply placed in the appropriate box – one for hackles, one for furs, one for tinsels & threads etc. Card index drawers and other types of office storage systems can also be used and are often available second hand at low cost. Exactly how you divide and separate different materials is entirely up you – so long as you are able to find things easily.

TWO WORDS OF WARNING

Parasitic Infestation

In the wild, most birds and wild animals carry natural infestations. These infestations can prove a serious problem once imported into the home environment. Feather mites can ravage and render useless a collection of fur and feather in a few days. It is strongly advised therefore that any plumage or fur which is brought in from the outside is dried and placed in a sealed bag, preferably with some Naphthalene crystals (moth balls) and kept in 'quarantine' away from your other materials. This can be checked from time to time, and at the first sign of any infestation, disposed of. Hesitate at your cost! Fur acquired from 'roadkills' should be skinned, washed and cured immediately, and stored as described.

Rabies

Those fortunate enough to live in countries free of rabies really never consider the horror of this virus. Caution should be exercised even if the temptation to pick up a roadkill is overwhelming. The rabies virus lives in saliva and nerve and brain tissue, and is usually transmitted by a bite. However, the virus can live on even after the death of the animal. It normally survives only a few hours in warm weather, but this period can run into days. If frozen, it can survive for two weeks and is able to become active again when the animal is thawed out.

For those determined to collect from roadkills, a pair of rubber gloves should be part of the kit at all times. Clorox kills the virus on contact, so drench the animal in this before setting about removing its skin. If it has gone into the freezer, it should be left untouched for at least a month. Apart from the above general observations, tyers wanting to pick up roadkills in areas where rabies is endemic would be well advised to take advice from the local veterinary practitioner before even contemplating collecting materials.

SHRIMP – a sub-surface imitator

MATERIALS

HOOK: Heavyweight grub hook size 8-14

THREAD: Medium olive 6/0

WEIGHT: Flat lead strip

SHELLBACK: A strip of polythene 2-3mm (1/8") wide

RIB: Fine gold wire

BODY: Medium olive seal's fur, or substitute

HACKLE: Medium olive hackle fibres

The freshwater shrimp can be found in waters of all kinds, both still and running, in all parts of the world. It forms one of the staple diet items for trout and grayling, especially in the early season. For this reason, having a good shrimp imitation to hand has always been important. The pattern we have illustrated is a good close copy.

The colour of shrimp can vary from pink and fawn, through greenish-grey to shades of olive. The colours used in tying this fly can obviously be adjusted to reflect these variations.

In this dressing, Polythene is used as a shell back to represent the shiny shell of the natural. Other materials are often used, probably the most popular types being Spectraflash or similar materials. These materials, usually available in sheet form, have an iridescent surface-effect in various colours and are ideally suited to imitations which will be used in coloured or fast flowing water, the extra flash making the fly more visible to the trout.

There are many minor variations to shrimp patterns: some have short tails etc., but many of them share the main features of this pattern – a dubbed straggly hair body

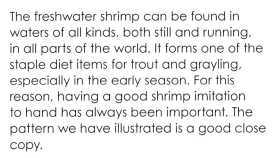

which imitates the legs of the shrimp, a stretched back which imitates the shell back of the natural and a ribbing which is used to represent the body segmentation present in the natural shrimp.

Other variations include the use of red or orange dubbing in the centre of the body to imitate the red haemoglobin glow from within the shrimp's internal organs. The Traun Red Spot Shrimp shown above is a very good example of this; it also uses Spectraflash for the shell back.

Apart from rainbow and brown trout, shrimp patterns are also deadly when fishing for grayling.

SHRIMP – a sub-surface imitator

Step-by-Step Tying Instructions

STEP 1

Set the hook in the vice, taking hold only of the bend of the hook. From a position about 2mm behind the eye, run the thread back to a point above the barb, in close touching turns, and then back again to the starting position.

STEP 2

Lightly smear the hook shank with a drop of superglue and then offer the lead strip up to the top of the hook. Bind the lead down working back towards the bend. At the end of the thread, bend the lead strip forwards and bind it down back towards the head. Do this about 3 or 4 times, making each layer of lead shorter than the last to produce a humped shape.

STEP 3

When the lead application is finished, cover it completely with a layer of thread to even out any lumps and to produce an evenly tapered, humped body, leaving the thread at the rear position.

STEP 4

The next step is to tie in a length of gold wire for the ribbing. This is then followed by the polythene strip.

STEP 5

The following procedure is explained in detail on page 48, **The Dubbing Loop**. Form a loop in the thread about 10cm (4") long and then take the thread up to the position behind the eye. A dubbing twister should then be set in the loop to hold it open. Lightly wax the thread on the inside of the loop (there should be no lumpy residue on the thread).

Tease out the seal's fur and apply it along the inside of the loop – in this case you can afford to be quite generous with the amount. Try to spread the dubbing mixture out evenly. Now take hold of the dubbing twirler between thumb and forefinger and give it a spin. This spinning will trap the applied dubbing between the two strands of thread and produce a hairy 'rope'. The dubbed body of the shrimp should have plenty of straggly hairs to give life and movement.

STEP 6

The next step is to wind the dubbing rope forwards in even turns. Take the end of the dubbing rope in the hackle pliers. Once this is done, the rope can no longer untwist and the twirler may be removed. Take the dubbing forward in even turns until you reach the front position. Take a couple of turns with the tying thread to secure the rope and then cut away the excess.

STEP 7

Now take hold of the polythene and stretch it forwards over the back of the shrimp quite tightly. At the front position take several turns of thread over the polythene to secure it and cut away the excess. Wrap the ribbing forward in open turns, pulling it quite tightly into the back to divide it into segments. Work the wire backwards and forwards as you do this so that the minimum amount of dubbing is trapped. At the head, secure with the tying thread and remove the waste.

STEP 8

Select a bunch of cock hackles and tie them under the hook shank as a beard hackle. Take two or three turns of thread to secure the hackle and then trim away the excess stalks. Finally take some turns of thread to build up a small, neat head. The tying thread should then be made secure with several whip finish turns or half-hitches. A drop of varnish will finish of the fly.

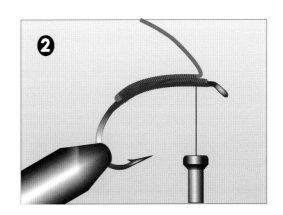

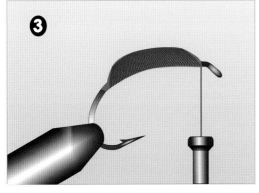

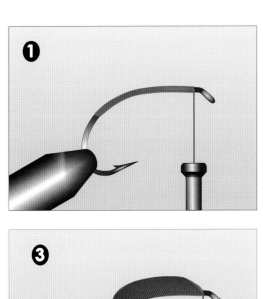

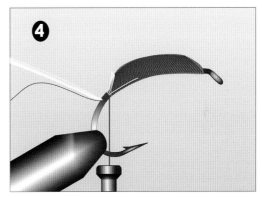

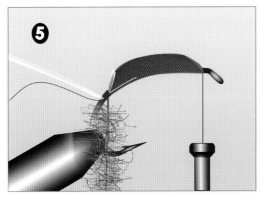

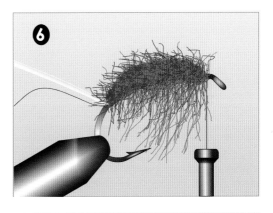

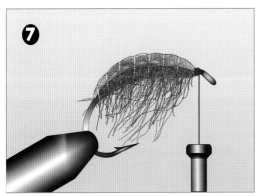

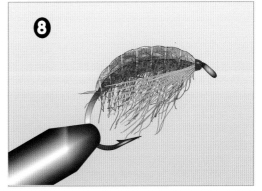

TRICKS OF THE TRADE 11: CAPE COLOURS

One of the areas of flytying that causes a great deal of confusion among newcomers is the naming and description of colours. Generally, natural colours are not the solid, bright, pure colours possessed by dyes and paints. The natural colour is usually more subdued and subtle. The most common names you will see are as follows:

Badger: This describes a feather with a dark central stripe and lighter tips. The centre stripe can vary from dark red-brown through to black. The tips can vary from pure white through to an orange-yellow. The tip colour is indicated by the qualifying name, e.g. a Golden Badger has tips of golden yellow and a centre of dark brown to black. A Silver Badger has a black centre and silver-white tips.

Blue Dun: This is an almost indescribable colour, from a brown-blue-grey tobacco smoke colour which may stretch to a mousey grey-fawn. The tone of the colour can vary from light, through to near black, the darker shades having a 'steeliness' about them. The following list goes from light to dark: light blue dun, blue dun, dark blue dun, iron blue dun.

Coch-y-Bonddu: This is a variation of a badger colouration in which the colours vary from dark in the centre, through light and back to dark again at the tips. The centre and tips are a dark red-brown, the colour between varies from ginger to a rich yellow.

Cree: This is a feather which is randomly marked with splashes of mixed colours. The splashes may vary from white, through ginger to a dark red-brown and black. The colour of the feather is normally nominated by the most dominant colour.

Greenwell: A special case of a badger colouration, so-called because it is used to tie the famous 'Greenwell's Glory' fly. A Greenwell feather has a central stripe which is very dark red-brown to black, with tips of a rich, orange yellow or ginger.

Grizzle: This term describes feathers that are coloured with regular vee-shaped bands of black and white along their length. Grizzle hackles are also available with brown and white banding. Grizzle hackles are one of the most often used of all feather colours.

Olive: This is a green colour with a tinge of khaki. It can vary from a light yellow through to a very dark green. The shade is described as light, medium or dark olive. Special cases are Golden Olive, which is normally a golden yellow, and Sooty Olive which is a very dark grey with a yellow-green tinge.

Red or Red Game: Natural red is not red at all, but rather a reddish, chestnut brown that may vary in tone from a light gingery colour, through to a dark chocolate brown. If a bright, pure red is required in a dressing, it will normally be denoted as 'dyed red'. The tone is nominated by a qualifying word, e.g. light red, medium red, dark red etc.

WOOLLY BUGGER – a sinking lure

MATERIALS

HOOK: Long shank lure hook size 8-14

THREAD: Black 6/0

WEIGHT: Fine lead wire 0.4mm (0.015") diameter

TAIL: Olive marabou with strands of olive Krystalhair

RIB: Fine gold wire

BODY: Olive chenille

HACKLE: Grizzle cock hackle dyed olive

The Woolly Bugger is a very successful American pattern that has proved its worth for Rainbow trout in many countries. The form is not a specific nymph shape but rather a general outline that can suggest all kinds of food items to a fish.

Woolly Buggers can be tied in all sorts of colour variations. The original tying was black but my favourite is the olive version which is shown here. Tied on a longshank 6 or 8 hook the fly makes a very good damsel fly nymph imitation, whilst smaller sizes may be taken for midge or sedge imitations.

Other colour combinations that are worth trying are orange, and black with a green hackle and tail.

The Woolly Bugger may be tied with or without the weighted underbody but the weighted version has an undulating motion during the retrieve which the fish find most attractive. It can be fished on all types of lines but is ideally suited to use with an intermediate.

The marabou tail has a mobility possessed by few other materials and together the combination of weight and marabou is a killing feature of many modern fly patterns.

The relative amounts of weighting and the length and thickness of the marabou are open to experimentation. Remember one important point about marabou – if you find that the tail is too long after you have tied the fly, do not shorten it with scissors. The sharp cuts produced by doing this create a totally wrong impression. Should you need to shorten it, pinch off the excess between thumb and forefinger to leave the ends of the fibres tapered.

WOOLLY BUGGER – a sinking marabou lure

Step-by-Step Tying Instructions

STEP 1

Set the hook in the vice, taking hold only of the bend of the hook. From a position about 2-3mm (1/8") from the eye, run the thread back to a point above the barb, in close touching turns. If a weighted version of the fly is required, bring the thread back to the front position and tie in a length of 0.4mm (0.015") diameter, round lead wire. Wind the thread back to the rear position, followed by the lead wire in close turns. Tie off with a few turns of thread and remove the waste material.

STEP 2

Select a bunch of marabou fibres for the tail. As a guide, the bunch should be no more than 1.5mm (0,060") diameter when rolled together between the fingers. The marabou should extend backwards from the tying-in position by the length of the hook. If desired you can add a few strands of olive Krystal Hair to add a bit of sparkle. Tie down the tail with a few turns of thread and return the thread to the rear position.

STEP 3

Tie in a length of fine gold wire about 10-15cm (4-6") long, followed by a length of olive chenille. To prepare the chenille, strip away the outer coating for about 3mm (1/8") to expose the core. Tie in using only the core and then bring the thread forward in close turns, tying in the butt ends of the marabou as you go. Stop at the front position.

STEP 4

Wind the chenille forwards in touching turns to the forward position, keeping an even tension as you wind. Secure the end with a couple of turns of thread and trim away the excess material.

STEP 5

Tie in the prepared cock hackle. This should be prepared and tied in as explained under **Palmered Hackling** on Page 21. The length of the hackle fibres should be a bit longer than the hook gape at the widest point.

After the base of the stalk is securely tied in, take the tip of the hackle in the hackle pliers and after taking two complete turns at the tying-in position, wrap the hackle backwards in even, open turns, keeping a steady tension as you do so. When you reach the rear position, secure the hackle with two turns of the gold wire and cut away the excess. You will find that between five and seven turns of the hackle is about right.

STEP 7

Now take the gold wire between forefinger and thumb and wind it towards the head in evenly spaced turns, trying to keep the tension on the ribbing even as you do so. The gold wire should cross the hackle stalk in the opposite spiral, trapping down each turn as you wind forwards. You will need to wiggle the wire backwards and forwards as you do this so that you do not trap the hackle fibres. When you reach the front, secure the wire with a couple of turns of tying thread and trim away the excess.

STEP 8

Finish the fly with several turns of thread, making a small neat head – do not overdo this. Make secure by either whipping or take a couple of half- hitches. Complete the head with a drop or two of varnish – do not use too much so that it runs into the hackle. Either use your fingers or a hackle guard, to hold the hackle back out of the way whilst you apply the varnish.

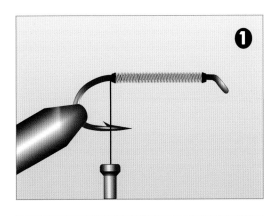

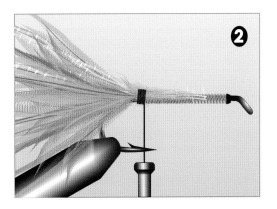

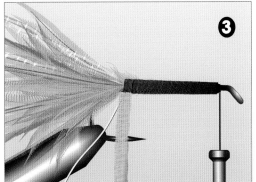

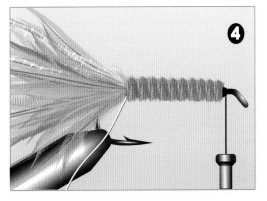

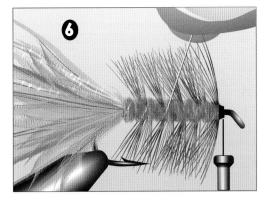

INDEX